D0286131

Self-love
guided journal

A 30-day journey of self-discovery and emotional healing to
help you feel good enough.

A Soul Scroll Journal
By Suzanne Heyn

*Understand yourself to create a life
as unique as you are.*

For bonus resources visit:
SoulScrollJournals.com/bonuses

© Copyright 2020 Suzanne Heyn

All content is original by Suzanne Heyn. All rights reserved.

Cover, layout and design by the Soul Scroll Journals team.

No part of this book may be reproduced, scanned or distributed in any printed or electronic form without permission.

For more information, visit SoulScrollJournals.com or email hello@soulscrolljournals.com.

You can also learn more about Suzanne's work at SuzanneHeyn.com.

DISCLAIMER

This book is for entertainment purposes only. This journal is not a substitute for therapy or professional medical or mental health advice.

Although the Author has made every effort to ensure the information in this book was correct at press time, the author does not assume and hereby disclaims any liability to any part for any loss, damage, or disruption caused by this book.

The Author and/or distributors are not responsible for any adverse effects resulting from the use of the suggestions outlined in this program.

Table of contents

Welcome!

I'm so glad you're here! You saying yes to this journey means you're ready for something deeper.

Deeper than bubble baths and flowers, chocolates and days at the spa that make you feel good momentarily but aren't lasting.

Deeper than attempts to improve or fix yourself, or be something you're not so you can feel worthy of love.

Deeper than all the outside things you thought would bring happiness but could never quite cover up the pain. The pain of not loving yourself. The only true pain there ever is.

Loving yourself gives you a certain boldness, a willingness to stop out into the world unafraid of making mistakes or messing it all up.

When you know that no matter what, you have your own back, you can go anywhere, do anything, live whatever kind of life you want to. It's all yours. The key to the universe. In your hand.

Before we get started...

I'd love to invite you to meditate each day because this is one of the most powerful ways of tuning into your heart and releasing uncomfortable emotions.

You're invited to try the Feeling Awareness meditation available for free at SoulScrollJournals.com/bonuses, or any other meditation you love.

The daily readings and prompts are for your mind, but a big part of the transformation is learning to experience everything you feel with unconditional acceptance. The Feeling Awareness meditation technique will show you how!

To introduce myself, my name is Suzanne Heyn, and I am the founder of Soul Scroll Journals.

I am committed to helping people understand themselves so they can create lives as unique as they are.

I've always been a person who feels things very deeply. A sensitive soul, I was born into a family that didn't understand emotions.

There was no communication, no felt love, no sense of togetherness. So when my father and sister died a year apart from each other while I was an early teen, I created a goal for myself: To appear strong and cold and never hurt.

Maybe I appeared strong on the outside, but on the inside, I felt sad and alone. I spent years at war with myself, wanting to heal my heart and connect with others, but not really knowing how.

Then, at 27, I developed breast cancer. This experience, which I believe partially developed because of my life-long pattern of repressing emotions, broke me open. For the first time in my life, I couldn't repress or deny how I felt. The emotions consumed me. People told me I was crazy when the truth was, I'd never felt more sane.

While healing emotionally from cancer, I learned to feel my feelings. I developed healing processes to help people understand why they are the way they are, which creates space for love and, if desired, the opportunity to create change.

Looking back, all my life doctors doled out diagnosis after diagnosis. None of them bothered to ask me — Do you love yourself? Have you learned to process the pain you're feeling?

Although many people are experiencing the pain of trauma, or the consequences of growing up in households with not enough love we live in a wonderful time where we have so many tools available for healing.

We have rich, nuanced language to help people put into words what they're feeling, to validate their experiences, and to help them heal.

This book is a book of love, understanding, a carefully designed journey to guide you home to the deepest part of yourself.

Please commit to the journey and spend time each day with the material. It's easy to resist, but lasting transformation waits for you on the other side. I cannot wait to hear how it goes for you.

Happy soul scrolling!

All the love,

Suzanne Heyn

Founder, Soul Scroll Journals

PS — Share your journaling experience on social media tagging #soulscrolling or @soulscrolljournals for the chance to be featured!

How to use this journal

It's best to carve out time each day to read the day's passage and journal your thoughts, perhaps in the morning or evening.

However, this journey is ultimately yours to do however feels aligned to your best interest. What's important is that you make it a priority, intentionally carving time out for it. If you skip a day or a few days, return to the work quickly.

It's easy to start with sky-high intentions, but you'll be facing things that feel difficult or even scary. You will stir things up that have sat dormant for a long time.

It's natural for resistance to show up, and sometimes resistance likes to convince you that scrolling your phone or watching TV is more important than scrolling your soul!

Show up for yourself. Creating change isn't about consuming information. It's about going within and seeing where perspectives and pains that don't serve you are controlling your life. The time has come to release them.

You're about to create powerful shifts that will forever change your life! The woman you are becoming thanks you for this. Take a moment to write an intention. Why is doing this work important? What will you tell yourself when you don't feel like doing it?

Bonus resources

Free meditation for releasing painful emotions

As you connect to your heart, things come up. Head to SoulScrollJournals.com/bonuses to access your free meditation to process what you feel and connect to your inner wisdom.

Join the Soul Scroll Journals Family Facebook group!

Personal growth can be lonely, but it doesn't have to be! Head to www.facebook.com/groups/soulscrolljournals to connect with others on the path of creating a unique, soulful life.

Week 1: Setting the foundation

This week, you're going to learn the most common myths of self-love and why they're holding you back from feeling good enough.

You'll learn the basics of how one who loves themselves thinks, feels and lives in broad strokes.

Later in the course, you'll explore these themes more deeply, but this is an important week of getting in the right mindset.

Day 1: Ready to shine?

This journey is about understanding that even with your so-called flaws, all the things you don't like, you're still lovable. Even with any outbursts and selfishness or brattiness and bitchiness, too niceness and resulting anger or resentment, you are still lovable.

In fact, the more you create space for those feelings, the very things you fear, the more you will integrate them into your personality. Once integrated, they will no longer control you subconsciously but instead become tools that you can use for your benefit.

Selfishness integrated becomes the love you have for yourself, reflected in how well you care for yourself so that you may fully show up for others.

Bitchiness or meanness integrated becomes the way you stand up for yourself when people treat you in a way that you don't like. Not from a place of cruelness, but from a place of firmness and standing your ground.

Love is all encompassing and has room for every part of you. The more you connect to the truth of this love within you, the less dark your darkness will become. But you'll never be perfect or have a perfect life, and that's not what this is about.

This is about deep, unconditional, radical acceptance of yourself and your life. That's the foundation of all positive change. Before you can live the life of your dreams, you must love yourself.

That's because your destiny, your life purpose, is distinctly you. It carries the stamp of your unique energy, and if you don't love yourself, you won't love what you create. Life is the ultimate act of creation.

Today, let's define what self-love is.

Self-love is very simple. Self-love is a relationship with your higher, true self. It's not something you do, or find time for, but a foundational way of interacting with yourself and the world.

Self-love is about aligning to your higher self and seeing your smaller self — the personality, the ego — through the lens of your higher self. This will help you accept your so-called flaws, understand your mistakes as necessary learning opportunities, and respond to any pain you feel with love.

Self-love is about dropping the judgment of yourself and instead working to understand yourself. It's about transforming judgment and resistance into compassion and curiosity.

Self-love is about noticing when you're judging yourself and then not judging yourself for that, but instead understanding that ALL pain — whether physical or emotional — is your soul, crying out through your body, for love.

Self-love is about a relationship to the universe and your higher self, a spiritual relationship of your own understanding.

How to connect to your higher self:

How you cultivate this relationship is entirely your choice, but a few options include journaling, meditating, spending time in nature, practicing yoga — basically anything that circulates your energy and allows you to feel that energy.

Even if you do cardio, you might spend a few moments afterward and notice that powerful energy circulating. Runners often report a runners' high, and at the most basic level, that's what this is — when the energetic body, a layer closer to the soul, becomes palpable to the physical body.

Discovering the practices that stir this energy and then incorporating them into your life daily is the process of spending time with your true self, which is also the process of developing a relationship with your true self.

It's about prioritizing your true self, so that you feel valued and loved.

It's an energetic state of being, and not one that involves a lot of thinking, and that's why it's so hard for many people to understand. You just have to feel it.

It's very subtle, but the more you can live from that place of connection, the happier, more peaceful and confident you will be. From this connection, it's easy to understand your magnificence.

During this journal, you'll work to remove the wounds and limiting beliefs that are the only thing blocking your natural radiance, but it's very important to begin cultivating a daily spiritual practice if you haven't already. The guided meditations at SoulScrollJournals.com/bonuses are a good place to start.

This is about caring for and nurturing your energy as a daily practice so that you can show up fully in your life.

Journal prompts:

Today, write a declaration of self-worth. Something like, "I am worthy of love. I am enough. I love myself unconditionally."

Whatever resonates with you. You probably won't believe it right now, but that's okay.

This whole journal is about *deciding* that you are enough and worthy of love, taking that knowing for granted, and systematically unwinding any thoughts, beliefs or habits that tell you otherwise. We'll go more into this as the journal goes on, but this is the foundation.

Yes, it's a leap of faith, but that's why it works.

Further questions:

What existing ideas of self-love do you have? How do you feel about those ideas?

In what ways do these ideas serve you and in what ways do they defeat you? What mindset shifts could you make to help you think about self-love in a more loving way?

How would you like your relationship with yourself to feel? What spiritual practices would you like to incorporate into your daily life?

_____
_____
_____
_____
_____
_____
_____
_____
_____
_____

_____
_____
_____
_____
_____
_____
_____
_____
_____
_____
_____
_____
_____
_____
_____
_____
_____
_____
_____
_____
_____
_____
_____
_____
_____
_____
_____
_____
_____

_____
_____
_____
_____
_____
_____
_____
_____
_____
_____
_____
_____
_____
_____
_____
_____
_____
_____
_____
_____
_____
_____
_____
_____
_____
_____
_____
_____

Day 2: Erasing the obstacles.

Today may trigger some people; I'm not sure! But it's an important lesson and the sooner you allow yourself to integrate it, the faster and more profound you'll shift. If you do find yourself triggered, know that only means there's great healing for you.

Again, this whole process is about tuning in with compassion instead of judgment or criticism. At the same time, it's important to have a sort of discipline, an edge to your devotion.

Love can be soft, but it can also be tough. Fierce. A willingness to face your fear because sometimes the biggest problem is thinking there's a problem.

We can be really attached to our wounds in a way that keeps the ego safe but doesn't allow the higher self to expand like it wants to. This attachment comes from not knowing who we would be without our wounds, pains and problems.

The universe is a boundless place and the feeling of freedom that comes from tasting that boundless potential can be terrifying. So we construct our own cages. And one of the biggest cages is the wounds we keep close to our hearts.

To heal, expand and grow, you have to let yourself let go. Let go of the pain, let go of the wound, let go of all the things that would have been awesome for you to receive from others, but you didn't. It's okay. You can still be whole. You are whole. All on your own. I will help you create a new identity beyond past experiences.

The biggest block to self love.

The biggest block is this: Thinking you're not worthy of love.

We're very attached to our stories of who we think we are. If you think you're not worthy of love, then you can't allow yourself to receive your own love because it would upend your view of who you think you are.

You can't allow yourself to experience something you don't believe is possible. Our deepest desires often come from our deepest wounds. We block the fulfillment of these desires, even the connection to our own love, because the wound of feeling unloved is part of our identity.

We don't allow ourselves to receive what we most desire because receiving it would mean that we're not wounded. And we believe we are. You can't love yourself if feeling unloved is a core part of your identity.

At some level, all healing is making the unconscious conscious. This journey is about noticing all the stories you have about who you are and dropping everything that doesn't serve you.

At some level, not receiving your own love serves you.

Maybe it allows you to hold out the hope of being rescued. Or maybe you hope people or the universe will see how you're suffering and change something about your life.

Allowing yourself to receive your own love requires you to suspend the idea of who you think you are and maybe create an entire new identity. It's about taking your power back and knowing that your experience of life is entirely up to you.

It's about making peace with the past and understanding that the things that happened to you aren't because you're unworthy. They happened as part of your soul's journey of learning, evolution and growth. Healing involves integrating these experiences to love yourself, the one who has experienced pain. When you feel unworthy because of the things you've experienced, transforming that energy into love for you, the one who has experienced them, dissolves shame and allows you to access the deeper wisdom.

Again this whole process is about deciding you are worthy of love and then systematically dismantling everything blocking you from experiencing that belief in your bones. But first you have to let go of attachment to the wound.

Be kind to yourself! This is deep work and a lot of it is unconscious. Your higher self brought you here to heal because you love you! And it's time to receive that love.

Journal prompts:

What pre-requisites do you have to loving yourself? What do you think you must do to be worthy? Where do you think those ideas come from?

How does feeling unloved / being hard on yourself / criticizing or judging yourself serve you? In what ways are you afraid to let go of that? Go deep on this one.

What wounds / stories are you most attached to? If they didn't exist, what new story about yourself could you write?

If you moved through life from a place of wanting the best for yourself, what would that look like?

_____

_____

_____

_____

_____

_____

_____

_____

_____

_____

_____

_____

_____

_____

_____

_____

_____

_____

_____

_____

_____

_____

_____

_____

_____

_____

_____

_____

_____

_____

_____
_____
_____
_____
_____
_____
_____
_____
_____
_____
_____
_____
_____
_____
_____
_____
_____
_____
_____
_____
_____
_____
_____
_____
_____
_____
_____
_____

Day 3: Love the mess.

One of the biggest obstacles to self-love is measuring your self-worth by how you feel. You may congratulate yourself when you're happy, feel like you have it all figured out, and then when happiness leaves, because it always does, wonder what's wrong with you. Why are you this flawed being who must wade through the ickiness of unhappiness?

I have good news for you! You are worthy regardless of how you feel. Happiness or even peace is not a goal, but a natural result of living an authentic life in which you love and accept all parts of you.

Painful emotions exist to let you know you're identifying with fear rather than love, living out of alignment with your true needs and desires, or that a deeper past pain is coming up for acknowledgment and healing.

Repressing painful feelings doesn't lead to happiness, but instead intensifies stress and suffering. Fighting your feelings leaves you fighting parts of yourself. The emotional energy you'd rather avoid doesn't go away when repressed, but only lingers. As time goes on, this emotional energy builds, creating more layers between you and your heart, making you feel more stuck, confused, off track, stressed and unhappy.

To release these layers, it's important to sit with your emotions. Feeling is healing. As you sit with this emotional energy, you are processing it and allowing it to release. This opens you up to the important messages contained inside your emotions — messages designed to lead you to your unique life. It also allows you to heal the deeper past pains and traumas causing you to feel not good enough. These unhealed past pains and traumas form the root cause of the bigger problems and patterns in our lives.

It's just a matter of switching your values. Instead of valuing happiness, which often reflects social conditioning that painful emotions are "negative," wrong or bad, value staying true to yourself. Your connection to yourself. This connection can be a much steadier companion than the fluctuating human emotional experience.

The most important way to love yourself even when you feel dark, sad or anxious is to recognize that when you feel that way, you need more of your own love, not less. This is how you create real peace.

Painful emotions aren't something to fight against, but messengers to let you know that some part of you needs extra love and assurance. Some part of you feels afraid, unworthy, or unsafe. Create that feeling of safety by tuning back into your heart, back into your higher self, asking yourself what you need, and then actually giving it to yourself.

The problem is not the emotion itself. The emotion has a meaning and message.

The only problem is the judgment. Feelings contain powerful information from your soul. Emotions are a sense, just like your fingers get hot if you touch a stove.

The messages of emotions are vast, but essentially sadness is something that allows you to release the past. It can also indicate that you're living out of alignment with your true needs and desires. Anger is a sign that you feel powerless, and can be a call to resurrect boundaries. Anxiety is at the core fear, a feeling of being unsafe or unworthy of receiving the basic resources — including love — necessary to survive.

Feelings of safety don't come from getting assurance from outside of you. They come when you can tap to that feeling of safety and security inside of you, which comes from tapping into your higher self.

Know that you can discover the messages of your emotions by tuning into the energy of them and asking what they want to tell you. An easy way to do this is in meditation. Download the free Feeling Awareness Meditation at SoulScrollJournals.com/bonuses to learn how to process your emotions.

A lot of people are afraid to feel their emotions, but that's because our society is afraid of painful emotions and the trauma that often lies underneath them.

Most people don't face their deepest pains. We're not taught *how*. That's why most people don't find true happiness. The more you open up to your sadness, the more you open up to joy. Meanwhile, numbing one emotion numbs all emotions. Know that peace lies underneath all pain. There's nothing to be afraid of. The fear of pain is greater than the pain itself.

Can you trust that your experience of the moment is okay because fundamentally, you are okay? There's nothing wrong with you. There's nothing inside of you to fear. Instead of abandoning ourselves when we need ourselves the most, we must respond with compassion and curiosity.

When feelings arise, simply breathe into them and start a conversation. Turn unproductive questions like, "What's wrong with me?" into loving questions like, "What is this feeling trying to tell me?" or "What do I need right now?"

When emotions stick around for a little longer, think of them as a cold, an energy within asking to be nurtured, honored and felt. Emotions are energy in motion; trust that they will move. Whatever you're feeling has an important message for you, even if the only message is that it's time to sit with yourself.

Responding to emotional pain with compassion is a foundational element of self-love.

Because this is a habit, it takes time to develop. When you catch yourself judging yourself, or attaching to the thoughts around an emotion, have compassion for the small self, the one who is suffering.

If you do fall into judgment or lose yourself in an unhelpful story, notice what's happened as soon as you regain awareness. Then, review what happened in your mind or journal it out, not from a place of criticism and judgment, or getting attached to the story of what happened, but from a place of curiosity and compassion.

Seek to understand your process, your triggers, and why you act the way you do. This is love! This is self-understanding and building a real relationship with yourself. As you become more rooted during inner turmoil using your breath, you'll more easily stay rooted during outer turmoil.

This shift can take time. Have patience!

Journal prompts:

What is your relationship to your emotions? Why is this relationship the way it is?

What are you feeling right now? What are your thoughts or fears around that feeling? Take a moment and connect to any feelings present. Lovingly, ask what messages they contain.

You might repeat this exercise for any predominant emotions you experience throughout life.

Next if desired, set the intention to connect to your higher self. Imagine a time when you were full of painful emotion, whether angry, sad or anxious. Write a message to your small self from your higher self exploring the emotion and why you felt that way. Open yourself up to guidance. Let your pen flow. Give gratitude for this connection and this feeling of being supported.

_____
_____
_____
_____
_____
_____
_____
_____
_____
_____
_____
_____
_____
_____
_____
_____
_____
_____
_____
_____
_____
_____
_____
_____
_____
_____
_____
_____
_____
_____

Day 4: Create loving thoughts.

Today is all about the mind. Yesterday, we talked about how emotions are always safe to feel, and I have the possibly controversial view that all thoughts are also okay to think.

There's definitely a helpful way to think, and I do believe in working with our thoughts, but I also believe this work begins with acceptance. We can use painful thoughts to unlock deeper self-understanding.

Requiring yourself to think positive all the time is essentially setting conditions or requirements for your worthiness. It results in denying how you feel, and valuing how you appear to others over how you truly feel inside.

Requiring yourself to think positive can also create a fear that you won't get what you want if you have a human experience. This creates resistance and fear, and experiencing resistance and fear around your thoughts and feelings makes them worse, not better.

Ironically, it's much easier to return to feeling good once you fully feel and acknowledge what you're thinking and feeling.

How does a person who loves themselves think?

1. Grateful.

Loving yourself is about fully receiving all the goodness in your life at the present moment. Be grateful for yourself, for the food you have to eat, for the clothes you have to wear, for the people in your life who love you. A good practice is to list five things you're grateful for each day!

2. Compassionate.

It's easy to judge yourself. What if you noticed that internal judgment, which is really the fear you're not good enough, and instead shifted the thought to something that felt better? Something like, *I know I made a mistake, but that means I'm going out of my comfort zone.*

Whatever you switch the thought to, just make sure you actually believe it. Don't repeat an affirmation that makes you go, *"yeah right."*

Before switching any thoughts, feel the feelings of pain or disappointment or fear underneath the thought. That will help you transition to a better emotional place.

If you're having trouble with this, don't worry. Know that it will pass and that it gets easier.

3. Curious.

When you notice a crazy thought, become curious. Instead of judging yourself, use the opportunity for greater self understanding. Ask, *"hmm. Why am I thinking that?"*

4. Solution-oriented.

If you're not happy with something, don't convince yourself that you should be grateful or happy when you're not! Take your concerns seriously, or nobody else will.

Speak up for yourself! It can be helpful when you have a problem to first come up with a solution before complaining or flipping out.

The other day, I was feeling really overwhelmed with work, my house was a mess, and the thought of cooking dinner was hanging over my head. I'm the only one who cooks in my house and even though my husband and I don't have kids, it can still feel like a lot.

I started to feel angry and resentful that I had to cook dinner. I started to judge my husband for not liking to cook. But instead of just taking this on as my fate, I suddenly realized that I had the power to shift things.

I couldn't change my husband... but I could order takeout! So I texted him and with a simple, "I'm feeling really overwhelmed right now and don't want to cook dinner. I think we should get takeout." And his response? *"OK."*

It was so easy. And in the old days, I would have spun off in so many ways, maybe judging myself for feeling overwhelmed, thinking I was selfish or not good enough for asking for help or having limits, or getting mad at my husband for being the way he is, which is a really amazing, imperfect person, just like me!

The key is to acknowledge how you feel, accept the situation completely, and then ask the universe to show you a creative solution of the highest good. They're always there. Acceptance allows us to find creative solutions that resistance or judgment blind us to.

Journal prompts:

Consider a problem or conflict you're experiencing. What is the story you're telling yourself about the problem and about yourself?

What is the truth underneath of those thoughts? Ask your higher self for an expanded perspective. Are there any wounds that need healing, conversations that need to be had, or perspectives that need to be shifted?

Feel and heal the feelings underneath those thoughts, if necessary.

If you feel called, write a gratitude list! Write one page of things you're grateful for, including all the ways you're amazing. Choose one of those things on the list and for 60 seconds, bask in the feeling of gratitude.

_____
_____
_____
_____
_____
_____
_____
_____
_____
_____
_____
_____
_____
_____
_____
_____
_____
_____
_____
_____
_____
_____
_____
_____
_____
_____
_____
_____

_____
_____
_____
_____
_____
_____
_____
_____
_____
_____
_____
_____
_____
_____
_____
_____
_____
_____
_____
_____
_____
_____
_____
_____
_____
_____
_____
_____

Day 5: How to live in love.

Today is all about living in a way that nourishes you, that fills you up from the inside out.

This whole journey of self-love is about connecting to the love within you, to your true self.

It's also about supporting the body, the container for your soul.

It's about entering into a relationship with your body and caring for your body as if you were caring for someone you loved!

To relish feeding yourself, caring for your needs, taking time to relax.

A lot of times the conversation around self-care is around the extras — the massages, the baths, the flowers. But even more important are the foundational activities include getting enough sleep, drinking enough water, and eating healthy food at regular intervals. Exercising matters. Doing what you can so you're not overloaded and overwhelmed by daily life matters. Focusing on your spiritual needs, like you are during this course matters.

These things matter. They're not extras, but essential. In modern life, we have neglected the soul, and that's why so many people feel depressed, anxious, detached and angry.

When these feelings arise, they can signal you've neglected your physical or spiritual needs. Neglecting your needs injures your soul.

This journey is about developing a relationship with yourself, allowing your body to know that it can trust you to care for it. This settles your nervous system, easing you out of survival mode and ushering in a sense of deep relaxation and peace. This relaxation comes from knowing you are cared for because you care for yourself.

Loving yourself is about recognizing that your greatest responsibility is to nurture and care for your own energy.

The more energy and vitality you have, the more you can enjoy your life and show up for those you love.

And in truth, if you don't care for yourself, or feel grateful for your health and do everything you can to preserve it, it's easier to get sick.

When I had cancer, it was such a wake-up call because I always felt that everything was my responsibility. I was a newspaper reporter at the time and ended up working late nights, well after everyone else left, because if there were spaces to fill in the next day's paper, I felt an undue responsibility to fill them.

But what I finally realized when I got sick — and I still need to remind myself of this — is that if I died, life would go on. Everyone would figure it out. The world doesn't begin and end with me.

And if I'm sick because I drove myself to exhaustion, I'm no good to anyone. I can't help people if I have no energy, no vitality.

So many of us sacrifice our well-being to care for others, but often it's because we want them to want or need us when what we really need to is to want and need ourselves.

When people really love us, they want us to be happy. Flipping that question around, do you value meeting others' needs more than meeting your own?

It's about realizing that you ARE serving others by serving yourself.

It's about understanding that caring for yourself and making yourself happy (while of course honoring how you feel) makes the world a better place because your happiness contributes to a happier world.

And if things are a little messy, if dinner is takeout instead of a home-cooked meal, if the dishes don't get done because you went to the gym, that actually makes the world a better place because it helps you show up joyfully instead of feeling grumpy, depleted, or less than.

Meanwhile, saying no to others gives them the gift of their own evolution.

You have one life.

You were born with a unique energetic imprint, unique perspectives and desires that will never be on this Earth ever again.

It's selfish of you to NOT devote yourself to your true expression. Otherwise you are denying the world of the gifts that only you have.

You can't offer your gifts to the world if you're depleted energetically. You can't offer your heart if you're disconnected.

To create a joyous, sustainable, compassionate world, we have to begin within.

It's time to take yourself seriously. Your desires, your needs, your feelings, your thoughts, your random urges.

It all matters. And the more carefully you care for each individual piece, the more the whole expands.

Over the coming weeks, we're going to explore all of this in greater detail, but today, let's just open the conversation.

Journal prompts:

What areas of self-care are you really good at? What need a little work? For those that need a little work, why do you have trouble? How can you overcome those obstacles?

Where are you taking on more than you need to because you feel like you have to? Where did those expectations come from? What fears do you have around shifting those expectations?

In what areas of life are you asking too much of yourself? In what areas of life are you cutting yourself too much slack?

What are your priorities in life? Does your schedule match your priorities? If not, what changes can you make?

_____
_____
_____
_____
_____
_____
_____
_____
_____
_____
_____
_____
_____
_____
_____
_____
_____
_____
_____
_____
_____
_____
_____
_____
_____
_____
_____

_____
_____
_____
_____
_____
_____
_____
_____
_____
_____
_____
_____
_____
_____
_____
_____
_____
_____
_____
_____
_____
_____
_____
_____
_____
_____
_____
_____

Day 6: Alignment is everything.

So many people live in survival mode, getting through the day and making do with what they have, perhaps feeling unhappy about their lives and not knowing how to shift. Taking the time to journal, feel into their desires and explore the root of their suffering so they can heal — this may seem like a Herculean task for which they don't have time.

This is the essence of survival mode. It's a reactionary state where instead of consciously designing your life, you react to what comes your way, creating an experience where life molds you but you are not activating your power to mold life.

The first, foundational level of happiness with yourself and life is about accepting what is and loving yourself no matter what.

Some people stop here, feeling like asking for more is somehow wrong or tempting fate. This is a fear-based paralysis, a prison based on limiting beliefs saying life can only contain so much happiness or that you're wrong, bad, selfish or greedy for continuing to expand. Making do with what you have is sometimes considered a virtue when really, that denies your desires, which are guiding you to realize your potential, which in turn benefits the entire world.

Creating a sense of acceptance is an accomplishment, make no mistake. However after cultivating acceptance, we're invited to continue expanding. To create a life limited only by the shape of our desires rather than one capped by fears of what isn't possible.

This is thriving. To unleash the desires of the soul and create a life that not only includes them, but is based around them.

Transcending survival mode into thriving is the ultimate act of self-love. It can seem like you're tempting fate. Will you allow yourself to rise up and sip boundless joy despite your intimacy with pain? Will you allow yourself to let go of who you've had to be to survive to become who you want to be?

Loving ourselves and maintaining peace of mind is about living the yin and yang — honoring both light and dark and realizing they could not exist without the other. Thriving calls for expanding our hearts large enough to hold bigger experiences. You've suffered. Now it's time to feel joy.

Today, let's talk about alignment.

Alignment is living in line with your soul's desires. This kind of life nourishes you instead of depletes you. It allows you to naturally discover and explore your talents rather than feel confused about what they are.

Not living in alignment makes your soul sad. One potential reason for emotional pain is untapped potential. Without outward expression, emotional energy can spiral inward and cause pain, fatigue or anxiety.

Find alignment by noticing how each interaction or activity makes you feel throughout the day. Energized or depleted? Satisfied or sad? Expanded or constrained? Peaceful or stressed out?

Just like emotions are senses from the soul with important messages, your energetic responses to people, situations and things teach you how to thrive.

The thing is, you know what feels freeing and what feels heavy. You know when your boundaries are crossed and when you're giving from love. That's not the problem. The problem is any judgment that arises causing you to perpetuate situations you know in your heart are out of alignment with who you really are. This whole process is about trusting your responses, knowing they are safe guidance.

Energy trumps logic.

Sometimes, a thing or person makes logical sense, but actually exhausts you. Part of self-love is honoring who you are instead of who you wished you were or think you should be.

From noticing how a friend makes you feel to noticing how your job leaves you at the end of the day, constantly assess how your outer environment affects your inner environment.

This isn't about being a victim to your surroundings. You can always change your perspective, and sometimes we must make do with less than ideal situations, but this is about the long term. Why try to make something wrong right when you can set the intention to find something that feels good?

This is about influencing your surroundings instead of being constantly influenced. Asking for what you need instead of just doing what others ask of you.

Returning to alignment when you fall out.

The thing about alignment is that it's an instant feeling of returning to center. It's a clicking in that makes you say, ahhh.

The more you live from this place, always noticing how the things around you make you feel, the more you'll notice when things feel off.

If you do feel off or sad or not as vibrant as you'd like, it's a call to review your habits and obligations to see where you can shift.

Are you spending too much time with technology and not enough with your heart? Is there a particular circumstance that's weighing you down? Did you say yes to something that's since become a no?

It's completely acceptable to change your mind. Following your heart means that sometimes things that seemed right one day no longer feel good the next.

Journal prompts:

Where in life are you doing things you think you should or that deplete you? Where have you compromised your true desires to make others happy? What beliefs do you have in place that inspired this commitment? What do you want to do?

What in your life energizes you? If you don't have anything, what do you think would energize you?

How do you treat yourself when you're out of alignment or feel off track? How can you better respond when you feel out of alignment?

As you move through the day, notice how your energy responds to each task, person and interaction.

_____
_____
_____
_____
_____
_____

_____
_____
_____
_____
_____
_____
_____
_____
_____
_____
_____
_____
_____
_____
_____
_____
_____
_____
_____
_____
_____
_____
_____
_____
_____
_____
_____
_____

_____
_____
_____
_____
_____
_____
_____
_____
_____
_____
_____
_____
_____
_____
_____
_____
_____
_____
_____
_____
_____
_____
_____
_____
_____
_____
_____
_____
_____
_____
_____

Day 7: Morning ritual.

Wow! The end of Week 1! It's been an amazing week of setting the foundation, getting in the right mindset and establishing some core principles of the self-love lifestyle.

Next week, we're going a layer deeper and investigating some of the patterns and beliefs you may have taken on from childhood that keep you from receiving the inner love you desire, or caring for yourself the way you deserve. Today is more practical! Your first self-love practice.

Morning ritual

The morning sets the tone for the entire day. A ritual helps you start your day peacefully, with intention.

My morning spiritual practice has become a sacred zone where I look upon my life from an elevated viewpoint. This helps me see the string threading it all together, and makes me feel supported, like I'm not walking alone. It gives me peace to look at life from a wider perspective.

The key for a successful ritual is to do it with intention rather than going through the motions because it's what you do every day.

My personal morning ritual includes waking up slow (I am not a morning person!), which means I essentially stay in bed until I feel fully awake. I judged myself for this for a while because society says you've got to wake up early and hit the ground running to be successful!

But my definition of success is making sure I feel healthy and happy, fulfilled and whole. So I stay in bed a while each morning.

I know this is not a luxury everyone has, but it's about finding ways to make your life work for you. Often we have much more leeway that we acknowledge. Silly rules about what we can and can't do tend to block us from taking full advantage of our freedom.

After I feel awake, I do a decadent morning ritual you can read about on the Soul Scroll Journal blog.

If you'd like to start a morning ritual and would love support to help you succeed, check out our yearly goal journal, Play with the Day, which features monthly intention setting journal prompts and weekly habit tracking spreads.

This process is what works for me, but it came after a lot of learning about what didn't work. A lot of habits others swear by didn't feel good for me. And some bad habits were lost along the way.

For example, I've long tried to exercise in the morning, but I'm low energy early in the day. Instead of feeling energized, I felt ready for a nap — even after yoga. Instead, I like exercising later in the day and find it gives me a good transition between the workday, letting go, and settling into nighttime.

And bad habits — I posted recently on Facebook about breaking my morning social media habit. Scrolling in the morning once inspired me but over time it no longer felt good.

First, it meant starting the day with the automatic reflex of reaching for my phone, which made me reach for my phone A LOT more during the day.

Second, it meant starting the day focused externally — literally reaching — instead of internally. This meant I much more easily fell into comparison without even noticing.

Starting the morning fully connecting to your heart and mind, fully grounding into who you are, whatever that means for you, sets a very important tone for the rest of the day. It helps you more easily notice what feeds and depletes your energy and helps you navigate the day more peacefully.

Great relaxing morning activities include reading or writing affirmations, making juice, drinking warm lemon water, doing a skin-care routine, journaling, reading or pulling oracle / tarot cards, or meditating.

When breaking bad habits, give yourself grace. Start incorporating small bits of good habits and celebrate each victory, even if it seems miniscule. New habits take time to create! Focus on moving forward in a positive direction.

How do you want your mornings to look and feel?

Maybe right now you're starting each day with this course, and that's great, but what about after the course ends? Would you like to continue journaling? Do you meditate?

The key to success is making your ritual sustainable, time-wise. In yoga teacher training, one guy had a 2-hour morning routine that he didn't have time for. We kept learning new things we *could* do, and he'd add them on, eventually spending all day just on his morning ritual!

At some point it becomes counter-productive. The intention is to choose one or a few activities that help you connect in and start the day in a positive way, living from intention as opposed to putting out fires.

Honor how much time you can devote, even if it's just 10 or 15 minutes, and also notice things you currently do that don't serve you. You don't have to start the day with the news, for instance.

Journal prompts:

How would you love to start your day? What obstacles do you experience that stop you from having a chill, intentional morning? How can you overcome them?

Why does this matter to you? How will it improve your life?

(If this doesn't matter to you, and it's not something that resonates, skip it! Although, it might be fun to give it a try and see how it feels.)

_____
_____
_____
_____
_____
_____
_____
_____
_____
_____
_____
_____
_____

_____
_____
_____
_____
_____
_____
_____
_____
_____
_____
_____
_____
_____
_____
_____
_____
_____
_____
_____
_____
_____
_____
_____
_____
_____
_____
_____
_____

Week 2: Taking inventory

If you have tendencies toward people pleasing, trying to check all society's (and your family's) rigid boxes and being "fine" instead of how you really feel, you are probably super disconnected from the truth of your soul.

That's going to change this week.

You'll identify and unwind your most damaging beliefs keeping you in cycles of sabotage — even if your family has been messed up for generations. Also get ready to learn powerful, easy tools to use for when you feel not good enough.

Day 8: Patterns of self-care.

Today is all about identifying ingrained patterns of self-care and self-love. We learn how to care for and love ourselves through our first caretakers, our parents. Our internal voice, the way we speak to ourselves, typically reflects either the way we were spoken to growing up or how our parents spoke to themselves. Our inner narratives are inherited.

Unfortunately if our parents had wounds, love they never received, impressions that their needs were burdens, they pass these wounds onto us. These inherited ways of being become the limited perceptions through which we view our lives. That's the bad news. The good news is that awareness creates the potential for healing.

A common wound is the mother wound.

The mother wound results from our patriarchal (male-led) society's denial of the feminine. Energetically, feminine qualities are those modern society tends to value less, including feeling, being, resting and relaxing. These qualities are needed to balance the masculine principles of acting, planning and leading.

Keep in mind we all, regardless of gender or sexual orientation, have within us both masculine and feminine energies.

Because of this denial of the feminine, and the devaluing of mothers and motherhood that resulted, many women have learned to deny their needs and sacrifice themselves for the good of others. Many of us have learned to distrust those parts of ourselves that are feminine.

This creates a war within, a sense that it's not safe to relax, to honor our feelings, needs and desires, or causes us to feel guilty for putting ourselves first. We rely on our inner masculine to keep us safe, but this cuts us off to important parts of ourselves, especially our deeper pains.

The mother wound doesn't only affect women (or men) who have poor relationships with their mothers. Rather, this wound is present to a degree in many people because our society's devaluing of the feminine has caused us to devalue those parts of ourselves.

This influences how mothers relate to their daughters, how women relate to themselves, and even how women relate to other women. Think of how much competition there is among women and how unsafe a lot of us feel in celebrating our successes. It's because the mother wound relates to a core feeling of unworthiness. We feel guilty for taking up space.

How does this present in your personal history? If your mom or caretaker consistently felt tired or overwhelmed or sacrificed herself — including her ambitions — to meet your needs, you may have consciously or not perceived yourself as a burden, perhaps felt guilty for receiving care your mother was unwilling or unable to give herself, or are suffering the consequences of having a mother who simply didn't care for you the way you deserved.

Any pain your mom experienced as a result of being cut off from her inner feminine was (probably subconsciously) passed on to you. As a child, you may have noticed her pain or resentment and sought to shift your behavior to pacify your mom, whose care you needed to survive. You may have begun to hide your needs, let alone desires, not wanting to feel like a burden.

As an adult, you may feel like you're not doing enough unless you're tired, depleted, stressed or overworked because this, to you, is love. Notice how you feel when you have leftover time, energy or money for yourself. How do you manage the extra?

To begin to shift, redefine what it means to care about something. What does it mean to help others while also supporting your own needs and desires? What feelings of guilt or pain come up for you when you think about this?

You might engage in this inquiry as a daughter (or son), but if you're a mother, take a minute to think about what programming or pain you're subconsciously living out. Where are you needlessly sacrificing? Do this without blame, but rather compassionate awareness.

Shifting this allows you to care without stressing. To receive without giving every last drop away. To help others from a place of overflow rather than depletion, obligation and resentment.

Healing requires first awareness.

Second, feel and heal any grief by honoring what you never received. Try the free meditation at SoulScrollJournals.com/bonuses to process your emotions.

Third, notice and re-pattern the ways this wound manifests in your life by deciding what changes you want to make.

And fourth, especially if you have a toxic relationship with your mom, it's important to create boundaries for what you will and won't allow in your life. Your heart can't heal if it keeps breaking.

This inquiry isn't about blame.

It's understanding that our parents can't give us what they didn't have. These pains are passed down from generation to generation until they're healed. This is a big deal. You're doing important work.

Any unmet longing for love or desire to have your needs met only comes from your parents' own unmet longing. They may or may not be conscious of this. It's not your responsibility to help your parents heal, but only care for yourself and take responsibility for how you show up in the world.

Maybe it even feels disrespectful to your parents to flourish because you worry that would deny their struggle. And if there was a sense of sacrifice on your parents' part, it can forever feel like you're trying to repay them.

If you're still looking for their approval, you'll forever sacrifice your own. There was never any debt to pay. Your presence alone is a gift.

Who do you need permission from to take care of yourself?

That was a big lightbulb question for me, and I realized just how much I used to quiet my needs. As a little girl, I once skinned my knee while bike riding and ultimately cleaned it up in the garage because I didn't want to bother my mother.

She's not a bad person. But there was a certain emotional frigidity that valued self-sufficiency and having no needs. My sister was called needy for asking for affection and I certainly didn't want that.

But our needs don't go away. Left unmet, our bodies react in other ways. Crying out with pain or disordered moods or other conditions.

To fill the eternally unmet hole of desire within, cultivate an inner parent who adores nurturing and caring for your inner child. Check in with yourself. A beautiful self-care affirmation is, "I delight in meeting my needs."

Sometimes we can deny our needs, as our inner child continues to wish and wait for someone to take care of us. But nobody is coming. It's time to heal.

Pay attention to signals from within that you need a break or water or sunshine or a few moments lost in a book. They matter because you matter.

Instead of saying: "No I don't need to eat right now. No, I don't need to rest. I can push through. No, I don't need help."

Say: "Yes, I would love to nurture myself by taking a break and eating some food. Yes, I would love to rest and honor my need to replenish my energy. Yes, I would love your help, or can you please help me?"

Needing help isn't a failure. It's okay to leave some things undone.

People who love you want to help you like you want to help them. Not doing everything for others gives them the gift of taking care of themselves. The happiness of others doesn't depend on your sacrifice. That's a story that's been perpetuated through the ages, fueled by the lie that women are inferior.

You are allowed to glow, to be happy and to receive everything you desire. You can care for yourself AND care for others. You don't have to choose. Your presence is a valuable gift.

Journal prompts:

What do you deny yourself? In what ways do you neglect yourself?

How were your needs responded to when you were little? How did that make you feel?

How did your parents care for themselves? How are you repeating those patterns?

If you took amazing care of yourself and fully honored yourself, what would that look like? Who do you need permission from to take care of yourself?

How can you look at whoever raised you through the lens of love, through the lens of knowing your parents were only acting out the wounds they developed as a child?

What does it mean to help others while also supporting your own needs and desires? What feelings of guilt or pain come up for you when you think about this? How can you see them differently?

_____

_____

_____

_____

_____

_____

_____

_____

_____

_____

_____

_____

_____

_____

_____

_____

_____
_____
_____
_____
_____
_____
_____
_____
_____
_____
_____
_____
_____
_____
_____
_____
_____
_____
_____
_____
_____
_____
_____
_____
_____
_____
_____
_____

Day 9: What is your archetype?

Today we're diving into archetypes and investigating how they influence our worldly interactions and self-care. Archetypes are roles or ways of being that are universal and help us understand ourselves more deeply.

Each archetype has a positive side and a shadow, or darker side, that left unnoticed can influence us in undesirable ways. Various archetypes will be present in your life. Because these tendencies are universal, they are present to some degree in all of us.

Use today's reading to understand more deeply how you show up in the world to receive love and explore how you might shift in ways that better serve you. If this topic interests you, psychiatrist Carl Jung and author Caroline Myss have written extensively about this topic.

The martyr

Being a martyr is about trying to receive love through self-sacrifice. The martyr feels responsible for the happiness of others while feeling unworthy of happiness on her own.

The martyr can evolve throughout life. For instance, I used to sacrifice myself — I became a newspaper reporter because I felt like saving the world was up to me.

Even after I "healed" that and moved on to pursue deeper passions, sometimes I still find myself making decisions based on what I feel like I owe people rather than what I actually want.

Ironically in martyrdom, we sacrifice ourselves, feeling like we owe the world and it's all up to us, but then feel like the world owes us for that sacrifice. We think, *I'm sacrificing so much, when will I get what I want?* We essentially use the sacrifice to subconsciously manipulate others into giving us love and feel resentful when the appreciation we desire doesn't follow.

Without awareness of what's happening, it's easy to head back out into the world to sacrifice ourselves some more rather than go within to understand the deeper patterns.

The true meaning of sacrifice is prioritizing what's sacred. Sacrifice can be fine, but only if it's inspired by true desire. Giving for the joy of it, and not with the intention to get.

If this is you, try to differentiate between doing things because you want to and doing things because you feel like you have to or for external love and validation. Returning to last week's alignment reading, tune into your energy and notice how everything feels. You don't owe anyone anything. Your presence alone is a gift.

The wounded child

We all have wounds sustained in childhood, no matter how amazing our families were. But sometimes, it becomes hard to release those wounds.

Clinging to hope that the past could be different, the wounded child continues to blame his or her upbringing for the way things are now. This carries a sense of defeat. Because of the way things were, this is how it must be. A common refrain might be, "If only this hadn't happened, my life wouldn't be this way."

Clinging to this narrative stops people from processing pain because the wounded inner child has an underlying hope that the past could be different, or that her pain will inspire someone to save her when ultimately we are responsible for our lives and our healing.

To heal, it's important to feel and heal the pain of your past to accept it, set necessary boundaries, and honor that your life can be whatever you desire it to be. It's safe to move on. You have the power to create any kind of change you dream of.

A lot of times with trauma, people become emotionally stunted at the age they were traumatized. So have compassion for yourself, allow yourself to be where you are, and begin to cultivate an inner parent who nurtures and loves your inner child.

Establish this relationship by creating space to connect to your inner child and asking what she needs, whether through journaling, meditation or simple conversation. Trust that you know what you need. It's only a matter of asking the question and staying open to the guidance.

Whatever is, is okay. You have within you an ocean of love that will carry you to the life you are meant for.

The healer

While the martyr is often thought of detrimentally, the healer is mostly considered positive. Healers help people remember their wholeness.

But in the shadow, the healer almost becomes a martyr, giving too much for the sake of approval. Healers easily become fixers, and end up focusing on helping others at their own expense.

Whether you become a healer during your journey or found yourself as a caretaker too early in life and end up deriving your worth from how you show up for others, this can cause an overly external focus at the sacrifice of the inner world.

The external validation from helping others becomes like a drug. Healers can drive themselves into the ground while helping others thrive.

Balancing this archetype requires setting boundaries and retaining energy for yourself. It can feel selfish to enjoy time or energy to yourself when you have so much to give. But if you give it all, you'll have nothing left for yourself.

You deserve to have something left for you. Please undertake this inquiry with kindness and compassion, remembering that all pain is a call for love.

Journal prompts:

How have these archetypes played a role in your life? What parts of yourself or your life do you feel you're sacrificing? This could be needs, wants, desires, anything.

In what ways are you holding on to pain in hopes that someone or something will change things for you? How can you shift this?

What do you feel responsible for in the world? Is this truth or perception? If you gave from a place of love and true desire what would that look like?

_____
_____
_____
_____
_____
_____

_____
_____
_____
_____
_____
_____
_____
_____
_____
_____
_____
_____
_____
_____
_____
_____
_____
_____
_____
_____
_____
_____
_____
_____
_____
_____
_____
_____
_____

Day 10: The power of self-perception.

Today is all about self-perception. Each one of us has traits we like and others we don't. The journey of self-love calls on us to accept our whole selves — the good and the bad — and lovingly evolve in ways that better serve us.

We must find the balance between doing inner work to evolve while celebrating how wonderful we already are.

This journey isn't about becoming a better you, but more of who you really are, the person who exists underneath any fear-based adaptations. It's also about understanding that each gift has a shadow, or dark side, and each shadow offers a gift.

Today, let's explore all of you.

What parts do you like, and which are you less fond of? What parts of yourself do you reject? How can you accept all of you while also creating space for growth? This is not changing because you think it's required to be loved or to achieve a goal, but rather living in complete alignment with who you really are.

You'll know evolution is required when something causes you pain or suffering. When things feel good and true to you, trust that feeling regardless of what the outside world says.

For example, maybe you're a wonderful listener, but feel frustrated at times, like others don't listen to you. Knowing this, it's great to honor your listening skills as a gift while also tuning in to when you feel yourself holding back from sharing your heart in conversation. You may feel called to commit to sharing more.

Or maybe you love that you're a dreamer, but tend to get stuck in those dreams and procrastinate on taking worldly action, and this frustrates you. Loving your dreamer side, it's important to also feel into how you can take more action.

Today, look at your whole self through the lens of love.

First, journal all the things you love about yourself for at least half a page. This can be personality traits, physical characteristics, things you've overcome or achieved, or just ways of being that you applaud yourself for.

And then write another half page outlining the things you wish were different. Things you want to change or improve upon.

This isn't about self-criticism, but compassionate honesty. This is about identifying those parts of you that you think you can't accept and learning how to accept them. Even be grateful for them.

After writing the list, look at each of these things through that lens of love.

For example, I really hate my feet. They have an abnormality that on my worst days, makes me feel like they're really ugly. I'm self-conscious about this and sometimes hide them.

But my feet are still my feet. They carry me so many places. They're my connection to the Earth, and having two feet means I have two legs! I'm alive. And healthy. And that's a big deal!

These days, I make an effort to show my feet love by rubbing lotion on them sometimes at night before I go to bed. This is actually a really nurturing practice to do for many physical and spiritual reasons, but it's also, for me, about taking the time to show love to a part of my body that's easy to judge.

This doesn't mean I necessarily like how my feet look, but it means that I appreciate this part of me because it's a part of me. I appreciate that my so-called flaws make me unique. Meanwhile, I have other awesome attributes like I'm a great writer and I'm really smart. Does that feel funny to read? It feels funny to write!

And that's why it's important to approach this from both sides. To acknowledge our flaws with love and to equally honor our awesomeness! Too often we hide the things that make us amazing because we're taught we shouldn't be over-confident or full of ourselves all while obsessing over the things we don't like.

We totally should be full of ourselves!

When you think of that literally, to me it says we're overflowing with our own energy and inner radiance. Don't you want to overflow with the inner radiance that magnetizes the right people and opportunities to you? That inspires and elevates others from merely being in your presence?

True confidence comes from expanding your heart big enough to contain both your amazingness and your so-called flaws. Arrogance and conceit aren't true confidence, but come from an attempt to cover-up deep insecurity.

Many times our so-called flaws actually create the pathway to our greatest gifts. Part of the reason I'm so passionate about journaling is because I'm a massive introvert who spent pretty much my whole high school life depressed and coping through journaling. Even during class! (My journal only got taken away once.)

I spent so many years feeling misunderstood by psychiatrists, but those years of psychoanalysis weaved a self-inquiry practice so deep into my being that I'm sure it's part of my destiny.

These painful experiences made me who I am and have led to a source of great joy — combining my love of writing and self-inquiry to create journals that I hope to help a lot of people with.

It may seem odd in a self-love journal to face all the things you wish were different. But a lot of times when we allow ourselves to really air out the crazy stories in our minds, they stop feeling so crazy. Often they're things OTHER people or society say make us weird, and we took that story on as fact.

When we resist the little nudges of "I don't like this" or, "I wish that was different," our insecurities take on monstrous lives of their own, limiting our happiness and sense of possibility. But these monsters are only figments of imagination. Our very refusal to look at them is what magnifies them.

Today at the core is about cultivating the courage to see your whole self through the eyes of love. It's about being totally honest and authentic with yourself, and from this place of courage, your inner radiance will shine, and you will feel the deep peace that comes from having met your whole self with love.

Journal prompts:

First, write a love note to yourself, describing all the personality traits, physical characteristics and parts of yourself that you love and adore.

Then, write the things you see as flawed, weird or unworthy.

Finally, look over the list of attributes you're not as obsessed with through the eyes of love. How can you see them differently? Write this down.

Find things to be grateful for or recognize ways in which your so-called flaws actually contribute to your greatness. Have compassion for those parts of you that you don't like as much and realize that they're all part of you. Fighting these parts leads you to fight yourself.

_____

_____

_____

_____

_____

_____

_____

_____

_____

_____

_____

_____

_____

_____

_____

_____

_____

_____

_____

_____
_____
_____
_____
_____
_____
_____
_____
_____
_____
_____
_____
_____
_____
_____
_____
_____
_____
_____
_____
_____
_____
_____
_____
_____
_____
_____
_____
_____

Day 11: How to slice through mean thoughts.

Today's exercise is amazing and important for the work ahead. In fact, this was originally scheduled for Week 3, but what you're going to learn today will support your remaining work during this journey, so I moved it up.

This journaling exercise will help you slice through negative thoughts and beliefs. In the beginning of this journal, I mentioned the experience was about deciding that you're worthy of love and then letting that decision teach you what you need to release.

Basically any thought or story that says you're not good enough or not worthy is a lie. You can spend all day long debating the mean voices in your head, or you can just declare it an untruth and move on with your life.

But we all know that moving beyond the mean thoughts isn't always that easy. They feel so real! You may also encounter limiting beliefs as you move along this journey.

A limiting belief usually begins with, "I can't because...," but limiting beliefs come in many forms. Did you know that perceiving mistakes as bad is a limiting belief? It's true! That blew my mind.

In the ultimate sense, any thought that doesn't come from love, pure love, is a limiting belief. It's limiting the expression of your true self.

The key for these thoughts is to honor them, let them exist instead of fight them, and then use today's journaling exercise to dissolve them in a deeper way.

This process will help you work through mean thoughts on a deep level rather than paste over them with a positive affirmation you don't believe. Affirmations properly used are powerful, but this inner healing work must be done first to address any pain.

Step 1. Consider an area you want to work on.

Since this is a self-love course, let's consider the idea that you are worthy of love.

Step 2. Write down all the reasons you believe this thought isn't true.

Spend time here and write as much as you feel called. It could be pages. So you might write: I'm a mean, horrible person. I'm stupid and never do anything right. I'm a total failure when it comes to my career; I haven't achieved anything meaningful....

The list goes on. Getting your actual internal narrative on the page is incredibly healing in itself. It may feel shocking, but that's why this awareness is a powerful move in the right direction.

Step 3. Go down the list and ask yourself if these things are ultimately true.

Sometimes, as soon as you write something down, it's easy to see that it's a total lie. It might even make you chuckle. Win!

Otherwise, begin challenging these beliefs. Is it true that you're a mean, horrible person? I'm guessing no. Because you're here, you have shown a sincere interest in growing the love you feel inside, which improves your life and the lives of others. Someone who is truly mean would never do that.

I've actually struggled with this belief a lot and have concluded that we all have meanness and kindness within. The determining factor between whether or not you're a good person is if you want to be good and kind.

"Good" is such a loaded word, especially for women, so we need to trust that we are innately good so we can be who we really are. Much of our power comes from allowing ourselves to embrace the parts of ourselves society says good girls can't be.

What if there was no such thing as a bitch? What if embracing your bitchy side helped you integrate it, supporting you in setting boundaries and putting your own needs first so you no longer felt depleted or resentful?

We need to trust that we're innately good and let ourselves be who we are, including those parts of ourselves we may judge as not good.

Looking into other possible mean thoughts, is it true that you're stupid and never do anything right? No! You're a really smart person who does a lot of things really well. First of all, not everyone wants to do this level of introspection. That says a lot about how intelligent you are and how committed you are to being your best self.

I bet you have many other amazing qualities, too. You're probably kind and compassionate and care a lot about making the world a better place. You do a lot of things right!

What if you haven't achieved the level of success you'd like? First, what you do in the world is irrelevant to how worthy you are of love. You are worthy because you exist! The more you dwell in that truth, the easier it will feel to give your truest gifts to the world, receive money and recognition for them, and shine!

Either way, I bet you're more successful than you give yourself credit for. You probably work hard, have a lot of great ideas and add your own unique flair to everything you do. You make life better for everyone around you, just by being you.

Essentially, all the mean thoughts are lies, lies, lies. Go down the list and challenge each and every belief. If something feels true, ask yourself, "How can I see this with love?"

Step 4. To go deeper, think about where this thought came from.

Where did the idea that you're not intelligent come from? What about the one that you're not good enough?

Connect to how that makes you feel, and ask your inner self to show you what needs to be healed. Some memories will likely pop up. Connect to the earliest one because it's closest to the root cause. A lot of times a seemingly random memory will pop up, but know it's definitely not random. Your inner self has shown you this memory because it has meaning for you.

Next, connect to the vision of yourself in the memory. Put yourself in the place of the younger you. Open up a conversation allowing your younger self to speak to you and you to her.

This is inner child healing, and it's one form of shadow work. Head to SoulScrollJournals.com/bonuses to access a free video with more details.

Let this flow naturally. You will know exactly what to do once you connect to your younger self. Feel any feelings that come up, and allow your soul's intelligence to guide you to a release.

Even if a memory doesn't pop up, simply feeling any emotions that arise allows you to release them. The SSJ bonuses page also features a free meditation to help you do just that.

As you feel and heal the feelings related to this memory, the mean thoughts will loosen their grip. After you've cleared the painful emotions, you'll have a much easier time believing more positive thoughts. More on that tomorrow!

You'll likely have to repeat this exercise many times, and often with the same thought, but that's okay.

This is a lifelong process that gets easier with time. Clearing the pain of the past isn't always easy, but it's always worth it. This is the work that allows you to believe in your unique gifts and live the life you're meant for.

Any time you feel fear about moving forward or are struggling to get out of your head, this is a powerful exercise to clear space.

_____

_____

_____

_____

_____

_____
_____
_____
_____
_____
_____
_____
_____
_____
_____
_____
_____
_____
_____
_____
_____
_____
_____
_____
_____
_____
_____
_____
_____
_____
_____
_____
_____

_____
_____
_____
_____
_____
_____
_____
_____
_____
_____
_____
_____
_____
_____
_____
_____
_____
_____
_____
_____
_____
_____
_____
_____
_____
_____
_____
_____
_____
_____

Day 12: Transcending the story.

Today we explore the power of story, and how significantly the story we tell ourselves about how our lives are unfolding influences the reality of how they unfold.

Of course we don't have total control over our lives, but we have incredible power. Too often, we're conditioned to play it safe, expect the worst or not get our hopes up, and the resulting stories we tell ourselves are disempowering. Today is about creating an internal narrative that takes you where you want to go.

What's your story?

A few years ago, I was struggling to make my dreams a reality.

I was blogging regularly but didn't know how to create a business around my passion. I wanted to create courses, but didn't know how.

When I asked myself, *who am I?*, the answer was: I'm a writer working to build a community so I can eventually create online courses. (Our identities are much larger than a job, but that's another topic for another day. :))

That's when I realized the source of my struggle. I was telling myself I would *eventually* create the courses that I wanted to make. The subconscious is very powerful. If we tell ourselves we'll eventually do something, that's not the same as doing something today!

Immediately, I changed my story. "I am creating awesome courses to offer to my community." Within a few weeks, I created the course outline and plans to launch my first course, a 40-day yoga practice called The Big Shift.

Changing the story creates space to change your behavior. How you perceive yourself influences how you act, which determines who you become. Often we wait for life to catch up to our desire, when life is actually waiting for us to take our desires more seriously.

After changing your story and actions, it's only a matter of time before the external world catches up. All change starts within.

This isn't about lying to yourself.

The goal of this exercise isn't to ask you to shift into a story that you don't actually believe. This is the danger of affirmations. They can make you feel worse about yourself if you don't believe them.

The good news is, this shows you where your work begins. Simply repeating the affirmation won't create change.

Instead, if you would like to believe something you feel resistance or negative emotion toward, use yesterday's journaling and inner child healing exercises to work through the unhealed pain and limiting beliefs standing in your way.

It's important to honor the feelings that rise up for healing without attaching to the fear-based story around that emotion. The story is not ultimately true. It's simply rising up from unhealed pain. It's coming up so you can feel and heal it. Releasing the pain allows you to change the story.

Not all limiting stories or beliefs will have pain associated with it. If there's no pain and you can believe a more empowering story, simply start repeating it to yourself as an affirmation whenever old thoughts arise.

But if there is pain, it's important to work through it. Sometimes it feels like it's taking forever, but this is your work as a soul. Trust the process. You will heal when you're ready.

Every moment of feeling is a moment of healing and every moment of healing creates space for a new kind of life that reflects the infinite, incredible person you really are.

Above all, work at your own pace.

Find a new story you can believe! Something that feels good and inspires you. That's the most important part — to feel good and be inspired.

Shift from "I hate my job and don't know what I want," to, "Maybe I hate my job, but it's a paycheck and I can find something I do love."

Or, "I feel so stuck like nothing is ever happening," to, "I'm honoring that I'm not fully happy right now. In my heart, I know this is an opportunity to grow."

"I hate myself and feel so sad," becomes, "I want to love myself and am committed to adding pockets of joy to my every day."

In a more action-oriented example, if you want to become a regular meditator, change the story from, "I'm struggling to create a meditation practice," to "I'm creating a meditation practice." This honors the natural back and forth that occurs as you shift identities.

For example, if you skip a day, it doesn't mean that you're not a regular meditator. I skip days meditating. Just like if you skip a day at the gym, it doesn't mean you don't work out.

The difference is that if you tell yourself you're struggling or that you can't do something, it creates an easy out for you to quit.

Speak the story you want to breathe into existence for as long as it takes until it becomes real.

After changing the belief, it's important to back it up with action, of course! But shifting the story creates a supportive internal environment to help you transcend limitation and live a life honoring your true potential.

Journal prompts:

Who are you? What is the story you tell yourself about who you are? How does or doesn't that serve you? To guide this inquiry, you might consider a specific area that you're struggling with.

What new story would you like to tell? What story do you want to tell about where you're going and what's possible for you? Write it down in your journal, repeating whenever you feel called.

As you bask in the energy of this story, you will be guided to the right actions to take.

_____

_____

_____

_____

_____

_____

_____

_____
_____
_____
_____
_____
_____
_____
_____
_____
_____
_____
_____
_____
_____
_____
_____
_____
_____
_____
_____
_____
_____
_____
_____
_____
_____
_____
_____
_____
_____
_____

_____
_____
_____
_____
_____
_____
_____
_____
_____
_____
_____
_____
_____
_____
_____
_____
_____
_____
_____
_____
_____
_____
_____
_____
_____
_____
_____

Day 13: How to be who you are.

Over the past two weeks, you've done a lot of deep inner work. You've explored (and challenged) your concepts of self, self-love, how you were raised and how that influenced you. Today I want to balance all this work of expansion with a gentle reminder of acceptance and love for what is.

The tendency is to fix ourselves or get so busy overcoming who we are that we forget who we are.

First, there's nothing wrong with you! We tend to view our complexes or neuroses as things to get over or solve, and while there is a sense of working with ourselves, problems have a way of unwinding themselves when we approach them with total love and acceptance.

It's a process. One with seasons of becoming and unbecoming. Seasons of angst and anger, and those of peace and surrender. Each part of the process is important and holds value. Your journey is yours alone. Navigating this tension between evolution and honoring who you are right now is one of the many balances of life.

At times, you may get tired of facing the same old problems over and over, and wonder when a certain issue will go away.

But the truth is, the core issues of our lives don't go away. They get easier to deal with, but you will likely investigate the same things over and over again, just in different and deeper ways. And that's okay.

The self-love journey isn't about fixing yourself or letting go so you can get on with your life. It's a process of fully accepting yourself and loving who you are so you can live your life right now.

No more waiting to be this perfect, healed person who will never make a mistake again. No more waiting to figure it out before you take action. Move toward your dreams now. Love who you are now.

I believe that our souls are born into our bodies, into our specific lives for a reason, with lessons to learn.

It's almost as if the first part of our lives involves getting hurt — because even if you had an amazing childhood with awesome parents, we're all messed up in our own ways. That's just life. And the second part is understanding all the ways that damage influences us and working with it so the pain no longer limits our potential.

This is a lifetime of understanding and the journey has meaning. Every step of it. Underneath it all is the core human journey of finding beauty in imperfection, meaning in the mayhem, purpose from the pain. Because this is what connects us all.

When we deny our struggles, we deny our connections. When we try to be perfect or only show the goodness in our lives, we lose the chance to experience an important part of truth.

God, the universe... These concepts aren't abstractions for the altar. They're a daily experience of transcendence to help us find peace even when everything is broken. They keep us grounded when everything is amazing because the only truth there is, is the truth of impermanence. I get swept away by the search for bliss as any, but real life is much more multifaceted than that.

This is where vulnerability and authenticity come in.

Vulnerability and authenticity are similar, but separate. Vulnerability is sharing the deeper parts of your heart in a way that makes you feel a little fear because it's exposing a part of yourself that hurts, a part that makes you feel unworthy of love.

That's why it's so scary, but shame thrives in secrecy. When you shine light on the secrets, the shame dissolves. You are never alone in your pain. Everyone alive experiences the same emotions, even if the circumstances are different.

If something hurts you, it matters. You deserve to have a space where you can share the truth of how you're feeling without judgment. You deserve a space to connect with others who understand or empathize what you're going through.

This understanding came from my own pain, of feeling isolated, depressed, like no one cared. My healing came through vulnerable sharing, and unconditional acceptance of self, and I'm here to create that same container for you.

Through pain comes purpose. But first, you have to feel it.

Authenticity, on the other hand, is expressing yourself and living your life in a way that's true for you. It's not necessarily exposing a part of you that causes you shame, although that can be part of it, but more expressing who you really are.

So instead of not sharing your opinion because it doesn't fit into the subculture you identify with, or not wearing something you want to wear because you don't want to draw attention to yourself, living authentically is about expressing yourself in a way that's true to you. Authenticity is about being *real.*

To live an authentic life, you must first be authentic with yourself. That's the work you've done over the past week, facing your darkness, all the things within you that you feel make you unworthy or wrong or bad and hopefully you began to see, well, maybe they're okay.

Because I may be stubborn or critical or a perfectionist or even high strung, but I'm also loving and compassionate and passionate and caring.

We are who we are because of everything — our failures and successes, strengths and weaknesses, flaws and assets. We are who we are — the good and the bad — because of the things that have happened to us. They carve us into the people we are, for better or worse. And everything that's happened to you is okay because you are okay.

No matter how bad something is, it's okay because it also gave you a gift.

It gave you the gift of compassion or deep-seeing or strength or wisdom. Nothing is all good or all bad, nothing within you and nothing that's happened to you.

The secret to unconditional love and acceptance is to widen your lens and see the whole picture, both in yourself and in your life. So today, I invite you to practice acceptance for who you are, what you've been through or are going through. I invite you to congratulate yourself for the deep work you're doing. And above all, have so much compassion and love for yourself, the one who shows up every day to do the best you can. That's it. Every day. Doing the best you can.

Journal prompts:

Where in your life are you pretending something is okay even if it's not? How can you shift that and express your true feelings?

When you think about telling others how you really think and feel, what thoughts and feelings come to mind?

How do you feel about your deservingness to have people listen to your true thoughts and feelings? Do you think other people want to hear what you think and how you feel? Why or why not? Where does that come from? Are those things ultimately true?

Where in life are you filtering your self-expression (including clothes, speech, home decor, etc.) and why? If you were totally unfiltered, what would that look like?

_____

_____

_____

_____

_____

_____

_____

_____

_____

_____

_____

_____

_____
_____
_____
_____
_____
_____
_____
_____
_____
_____
_____
_____
_____
_____
_____
_____
_____
_____
_____
_____
_____
_____
_____
_____
_____
_____
_____
_____
_____

_____
_____
_____
_____
_____
_____
_____
_____
_____
_____
_____
_____
_____
_____
_____
_____
_____
_____
_____
_____
_____
_____
_____
_____
_____
_____
_____
_____
_____
_____
_____
_____

Day 14: Accessing the energy of love.

Today let's talk about the energy of love and how it relates to the chakras, the seven energy centers located along the spine. Even if you don't believe in the chakras, they offer a really useful framework for understanding emotions.

You'll also receive your second self-love practice today!

The energy of love

The epicenter of love is at the fourth chakra, the heart, in Sanskrit known as the Anahata chakra. The color is green.

From an emotional perspective, the first chakra, the root, located at the base of the spine, is about fitting in. It relates to your family and earthly foundation.

Feeling secure in your foundation creates space for you to stand out and express yourself through acts of creation, which is the basis of the second chakra, located below the naval. The second chakra also relates to emotions, and your ability to flow through them.

The third chakra at the naval relates to personal power, will and boundaries. Secure in your foundation and connected to your feelings as a guidance, boundaries offer containers for your life force energy to flow.

Physically, a strong body supports your ability to stand strong in the world. If you're having trouble exerting your will or creating change, consider strengthening your body.

Related to love, a strong sense of personal power and boundaries protects your open heart, allowing you to love while maintaining a strong sense of self. If your heart is too vulnerable or open without anything to protect it, it's easy to get hurt or sacrifice your needs and desires in an effort to receive affection.

But boundaries that are too firm prevent love from pouring in to your life. Anger relates to the third chakra, an emotion that asks us to create new boundaries and reclaim our power. Power struggles of the third chakra can also block our ability to give and receive love.

Meanwhile the fifth chakra, at the throat, relates to speaking your truth. So, secure in your foundation, in tune with your feelings, assured in your personal power, and connected to the love in your heart, you're able to express yourself.

Authentic self-expression carries all of these qualities. This is how you can ask for what you need from an empowered place that's still loving.

It's all about taking time to get centered in who you are, what you need, and your innate deservingness to have your needs met (while being capable of meeting them yourself) that allows you to speak your truth from a place of love.

But when you're learning how to love yourself, you may spend time debating your inherent worthiness.

You may wonder things like:

- Do I deserve to receive the things that I want just because I want them?
- I *could* do with less, so maybe I should just stay quiet.

- I feel so bratty asking for what I want! It's okay. I don't mind putting up with what's happening. As long as others are happy.

But when you consider this from the divine perspective, it's easy to see that humans were born to climb this energetic ladder. We deserve to have our basic needs met, to fulfill our desires, to set boundaries and speak our minds.

It's our destiny and part of the journey to self-actualization. You embodying your highest truth supports the continual unfolding of the world into its fullest expression. When you hide yourself, not feeling worthy of the divine potential that's in you, you not only stunt your evolution, but the evolution of the universe.

So if you tend to sacrifice your needs and desires for the sake of others, ask yourself why that is. Maybe you don't feel secure in your foundation. Or maybe you worry others will leave you or not love you. Perhaps you give your power away in exchange for love, or hide your truth because you fear it isn't nice enough.

The good news is that since these energy centers are wholly contained within us, we can find everything we need within. Even if you didn't grow up feeling loved, you can heal and connect to your own strong foundation, connect with the Earth to feel supported and loved.

Once you own who you truly are, you may leave behind people who loved the fake version of you, but in time you'll find those enamored with the real version.

Receiving love for who you truly are feels satisfying in a way that pretending never will.

A self-love practice to open your heart.

Today is my favorite restorative yoga pose. It's a great way to open your heart or support your body after a day spent at a desk.

Find two yoga blocks, a rolled up towel or rolled up yoga mat. If you're working with the rolled up towel or mat, place this underneath your shoulder blades, parallel to your arms. Simply lie on top of the roll.

If it's too much, unroll the mat/towel to create a smaller roll. If it's not enough, find something thicker. Make sure the neck feels okay. If it doesn't, rest your head on a pillow.

For the yoga block option, place one underneath the shoulder blades and the second underneath your head.

Start with both blocks on the lowest levels and adjust as desired. Lifting your head higher makes the pose less intense.

Then, hang out for a few moments while listening to heart chakra music. Wonderful playlists can be found on Spotify or Youtube.

Journal prompts:

How do the boundaries (or lack thereof) in your life support or block the giving and receiving of love?

How do you navigate the balance between love and power in your life?

How can you make yourself feel more safe so you can love more?

What things from the past do you need to heal or release in order to feel good about making theses changes?

_____
_____
_____
_____
_____
_____
_____
_____
_____
_____
_____
_____
_____
_____
_____
_____
_____
_____
_____
_____
_____
_____
_____

_____
_____
_____
_____
_____
_____
_____
_____
_____
_____
_____
_____
_____
_____
_____
_____
_____
_____
_____
_____
_____
_____
_____
_____
_____
_____
_____
_____
_____
_____

Week 3: Reclaiming your power

This week, you'll reclaim those parts of yourself you've compromised in an effort to fit in. You'll connect to your values and what truly matters to you so you can create a fulfilling life centered around those things.

We'll explore setting boundaries and the difference between being nice and being kind.

Ultimately, this week is about embracing who you are and making your life an authentic reflection of this unfiltered self-expression.

Day 15: Reclaiming the lost pieces.

Over the last two weeks, you've dug deep and begun to reset your ideas of who you think you are and what you must do to receive love.

This week you're going to discover more about who you are and feel into creating a life around that unfiltered self-expression. Ready? Let's go!

How have you compromised your true self over the years?

What personality traits have you hidden thinking they're too much or not enough? How can you re-activate them?

Celebrating these parts of you is essential for your life to feel good. Being all of who you are is important if you want to align with your unique life path, including living your purpose and finding true soul relationships.

For example, I'm a big introvert, but I love to socialize. Lots of alone time allows me to show up as my best with others. I used to judge my introversion, which separated me from my higher self and caused loneliness. (The true source of loneliness is feeling disconnected from yourself.)

Before, instead of connecting with myself, who I felt was unworthy alone, I tried desperately to validate myself through friends.

Because I wasn't centered in who I was, I connected with people from a place of insecurity. The relationships felt unbalanced and unfulfilling. To connect with others who resonate on a soul level, we must first connect to and love ourselves at the soul level. We must be who we are and trust that everything we desire will flow to us from this place of authentic self-expression.

In this example, feeling rejected by others created even more loneliness and desperation, fueling a relentless cycle that continued to make me feel unworthy.

Connection from a place of inadequacy never feels like enough.

When you're not operating in the world from your true self, nothing fits. We judge our true selves, thinking them not enough, and try to play the role of someone we think will be worthy of love or worthy of getting what we want. We connect with others, find jobs and create lives while playing this role, but nothing satisfies.

Because nothing satisfies, we try harder to shove ourselves into a box, trying to be who we think we need to be to get what we want, feeling more miserable all the time because everything feels stifling and hard. Instead of questioning the way we're living, we question ourselves, wondering why we are not enough.

The problem is not that you are not enough —you are so very much enough. The problem is the paradigm. Creating a life that fills every crevice of your unique heart requires honoring every crevice of your unique being. To find our true path, we must be our true selves.

Being yourself, allowing yourself to exist exactly as you are, is the foundation of feeling nourished from within.

I also want to mention that part of the reason I judged my introversion was because my parents valued social interaction, even though oddly they were not that social.

Perhaps this was projection on their part. If they judged their introversion and didn't accept it, it would make sense they would judge this quality in me. My sister was the social one, and I perceived that they approved of her more than me, and this caused even deeper pain.

I thought I had to be outgoing to be worthy of love, and so in college, I ended up drinking to be that outgoing person. I considered that outgoing me the "real" me, even though in hindsight, that was just the me I wanted to be.

It took a long time to learn how to honor my introversion, accept and love myself for exactly who I am. But deeper, accepting something I thought was a flaw allowed me to open up to my gifts, my love for deep thinking and sharing my ideas with others. That's just one example, of course.

Maybe you have a really loud voice but have been judged for that and have tried to quiet down. Or maybe you're really sensitive but have always been told that you're too sensitive. So instead of allowing yourself to feel and learning how to navigate that in a healthy way, you repress this innate sensitivity.

Repressing our innate nature not only closes us off to its gifts, but also makes it spiral out of control and ultimately sabotage us.

So today, accept and honor all parts of you. Invite the lost pieces to return. Every inch of you is a gift. It's time you allowed yourself to receive it.

What to do when you feel rejected:

It would be great to be your true self and to have life unfold perfectly. But living fully involves rejection. That's why it's so scary. It's worth it, but rejection happens, and it hurts. So what do you do?

Step 1. Feel the feeling of rejection.

That's the scariest part, feeling something you don't want to feel. But this is how you reclaim your power. The real pain of rejection is when we reject ourselves. We don't process the feeling when we believe the story around it is true. When we believe the story, we're not fully aware of it. Creating awareness allows you to create space to see the truth. So feel the emotion. Honor it. Let it move through you. Know the story is NOT true.

You may feel called to investigate this feeling using the shadow work practices described earlier, connecting to an earlier situation that possibly created beliefs causing your current pain. Visit SoulScrollJournals.com/bonuses for a free video with more detail about this practice and a guided meditation to help you release the emotion.

Step 2. Separate the feeling of rejection from the thoughts around the rejection.

You might notice thoughts like, "I'm such a loser. I never do anything right. Why did I try this stupid self-love stuff anyway?"

Options include journaling it out, getting back into your body, taking a walk, or anything else to help you move through. Focus on feeling the feelings and nurturing yourself through the pain while detaching from the thoughts rather than turning against yourself or abandoning yourself in judgment. When the feeling passes, the thoughts will dissipate.

Separating thought from feeling and allowing yourself to feel without getting swept away takes practice. Keep trying! You'll get better at it.

Step 3. Put it in perspective.

Understand the truth of what's happening. It's not that you're wrong or bad or unworthy. It's that you feel pain from rejection and this is causing you to doubt yourself.

The old you would have felt this pain and allowed it to influence how you show up in the world. The gift of awareness is that you can notice the pain, honor it, release the story around it, and remember that you're awesome as you are.

This is a time to double down on who you are. Back yourself. Have faith that if you stay true to yourself everything will work out. You're literally forming new neural pathways! This is all part of the process.

Journal prompts:

What parts of your personality were rejected when you were little, either by your family, teachers, other kids, or other authority figures? How did that influence you?

What gifts do these pieces contain?

In what ways have you compromised or conformed who you are to please others? How can you create space for those parts of you to emerge?

What characteristics of yours do you not feel connected to, but feel responsible for cultivating because of family or social expectations?

Consider writing a love note to the parts of you that you've judged, repressed, or hidden. Welcome these pieces of you back into your life and celebrate who you are, in your wholeness.

You don't have to investigate all these questions! Follow your intuition and just write whatever comes out. Whatever is, is perfect.

_____
_____
_____
_____
_____
_____
_____
_____
_____
_____
_____
_____
_____
_____
_____
_____
_____

_____

_____

_____

_____

_____

_____

_____

_____

_____

_____

_____

_____

_____

_____

_____

_____

_____

_____

_____

_____

_____

_____

_____

_____

_____

_____

_____

_____
_____
_____
_____
_____
_____
_____
_____
_____
_____
_____
_____
_____
_____
_____
_____
_____
_____
_____
_____
_____
_____
_____
_____
_____

Day 16: Discovering what's important.

A big part of loving who you are is spending time getting to know yourself. An important part of this is identifying your core values. A values-based life feels meaningful. Knowing your values and living by them helps you feel confident and rooted in who you are. It also helps you stand up for yourself and easily create boundaries.

Values are different than desires.

Today's conversation isn't about specific desires, which we'll get to later, but more about identifying what makes your life meaningful.

Desires are things you want while values are things with meaning. Sometimes they coincide and sometimes they're different.

We're covering values before desires for an important reason. Values tend to be more soul based while desires tend to be more ego based. Sometimes, we neglect our values — and our soul — while trying to achieve desires.

For example, our ego may crave climbing the career ladder, and while there's outwardly nothing wrong with that, if not checked by the soul, we may run right over what truly matters to us in pursuit of some outside thing we think will make us happy.

We may neglect our health, relationships and overall sense of joy while pursuing things outside of ourselves. You may acquire your desire, but find your life has no meaning because it's not based in a value.

Values help you connect to a happiness that's deeper than happiness based on desire.

Sometimes, we subconsciously punish ourselves for not having the things we want in our lives.

Like if you stop yourself from enjoying food or nature or vacations because life doesn't look the way you want. Maybe you don't have the body or the relationship or career that you think would make you happy.

In these cases, sometimes what's really causing pain is not the absence of the thing we've attached our happiness to, but the act of depriving our soul from its true, deep needs. Its values.

Ironically, what happens is we notice this unhappiness, blame it on the thing we think is missing, and double down in an effort to achieve something outside of ourselves. This leads to more suffering in a vicious cycle.

Sometimes what we really need is to take a step back and ask ourselves if our lives truly match our values. Nourishing the soul with a value-based life creates balance and harmony.

How to live a values-based life:

Step 1. Use your values to make decisions.

Once you know your values, use them to organize your day or guide your decisions.

For example, if you value family time, then it becomes easier to take the less demanding job, even if it means a pay cut.

If you value freedom, then maybe you pursue a telecommuting job or building your own business. And if you value adventure, then inspire yourself to actually take the road trip or vacation instead of just dreaming about it! You might also consider injecting more adventure into your day-to-day life. What would that look like?

Step 2. Use values to organize your day.

If it's important to you to write a book, then create time in your day to write the book! You might worry that your house isn't clean enough or that you're not cooking fancy enough dinners or any number of things. These things that seem urgent are often not important.

I've heard many successful people say their huge projects were accomplished in five-minute increments. Spending even five minutes a day on something that really matters to you will add up over time.

Step 3. Use values to establish boundaries.

Tomorrow's discussion goes deeper into boundaries, but if something is important to you, then it's important that others in your life respect that.

This isn't about requiring that everyone around you buy into your views, but more about respect and understanding.

For example, if you're a vegetarian but someone in your family insists on talking about how you're going to keel over without animal protein, then it might be helpful to have an honest conversation about how your diet is very important to you.

You can agree to disagree on philosophy, but make it clear that if this person respects you, then it's important they respect your choices.

Step 4. Redefine success using your values.

Success isn't only career accolades or money. A more holistic definition of success might include the ability to live a values-based life that nurtures you at the soul level.

A life that reflects the highest vision of what's possible. A life lived in reflection of your truth and not your facade. A life lived in faith and not fear.

Journal prompts:

1. Write a list of at least five things that it's important for you to be.

It's tempting to skip writing "It's important to me to be," over and over, but I find it helpful in cementing the ideas in the conscious mind. Obviously it's your journey, and you can do whatever you want. :)

Example: It's important to me to be authentic.

It's important to be me be happy.

It's important to me to be real.

_____

_____

_____

_____

_____

2. It's important for me to be known for _____. At least five times.

Example: It's important for me to be known for compassion.

It's important for me to be known for love.
It's important for me to be known for wisdom.

_____
_____
_____
_____
_____

3. It's important for me to _____. At least five times.
Example: It's important for me to eat healthy.
It's important for me to drink a lot of water.
It's important for me to get plenty of rest.

_____
_____
_____
_____
_____

4. _____ is important to me. At least five times, but preferably 10 or more.
Example:
Health is important to me.
Love is important to me.
Freedom (financial and otherwise) is important to me.

_____

----

5. Go through your list from No. 4 and begin with the first thing you wrote. Like you're at the eye doctor, compare that first thing with the second thing to evaluate which is most important to you.

Take the most important item from that first comparison and compare that with all the other things on your list, always taking the most important thing. This will help you find your core, No. 1 value.

Repeat this same process to find your top three to five values. If at any point you struggle to choose, just think about what you absolutely cannot live without.

6. Consider whether your daily life and current self-expression corresponds to these values. If not, what changes can you make?

_____
_____
_____
_____
_____
_____
_____
_____
_____
_____
_____
_____
_____
_____
_____
_____
_____
_____
_____
_____
_____
_____
_____
_____
_____
_____
_____
_____

Day 17: Setting boundaries.

Today is so important! We're diving into setting boundaries.

Boundaries are a matter of respect. They're lines that delineate what's appropriate in our relationships. Although boundaries influence outer relationships, they begin within.

As we respect ourselves, we teach people how to treat us in a way that honors the relationship, both with the other and ourselves.

It can feel scary to say no or have a hard conversation to set a boundary, but what's more scary is living life from a place where you're constantly energetically overdrawn or on the defensive because you have no boundaries to protect your open heart.

Boundaries also exist to protect what's meaningful, what you hold sacred. You might set boundaries to preserve your morning communion with self, just like you might have boundaries around toxic behaviors or the amount of time you spend helping others.

On the other extreme, it's possible to have boundaries or internal walls that are too high. Never asking for help or receiving support can indicate a rigid boundary that's intended to protect you, but more likely results in feeling closed off from outer relationships.

Overly restrictive boundaries typically result from fear or unhealed past trauma that left you feeling unsafe, or like you had to fend for yourself. They can come from a desire to protect yourself from getting hurt, from asking others for help and feeling rejected if they let you down.

Overly weak boundaries may indicate a desire to receive love from outside of you to compensate from the sense that you're disconnected from your own internal source of love.

The more you connect to the love within, the more you'll be able to heal the past and create healthy boundaries allowing energy to flow in and out while staying rooted in who you are and your energetic needs.

How to set boundaries:

Step 1. Use your feelings as safe guidance.

This is your life and there is no wrong or right. It's all what feels good to you. You don't need a logical reason for setting a boundary, although they will sometimes exist. It's based on how you feel, your values, desires, and what's necessary for you to feel good in your life and relationships.

Notice what makes you feel resentful or angry, and instead of judging yourself or wondering if you're selfish, honor the feeling. Seek to understand the situation.

Ask yourself questions like, "Why am I feeling this way?," and "How can I speak up for myself?"

Resentment and anger are powerful signs of breached boundaries. Anger can indicate you've given your power away while resentment comes from martyrdom, and the feeling that others' happiness matters more than your own.

Anger can also indicate the fear that you have to be someone other than who you are to exist in the world. Perhaps there is a tension, a push and pull between what you want and what you think is required.

This journey is one of making the subconscious conscious, understanding your feelings deeply, and using that understanding to create necessary boundaries in your life.

Step 2. Give yourself space to formulate a response.

Requests often come with a feeling of pressure to respond immediately. Just the other day, I said yes to something because I didn't want to disappoint another person.

In this case, I'll probably change my mind, which is always an option. Saying something like, "Let me think about that," is better so you have time to think it through.

Ask questions like:

- How does saying yes / allowing this thing make me feel? Why do I feel that way?
- What does saying yes to this request / allowing this circumstance mean I'm saying no to?
- How does this impact my time and schedule?
- Why do I want to do this? Why do I not want to do this? Notice the feelings that arise underneath that inquiry.
- What do I want to do? What do I think I should do?

Step 3. State your boundary clearly.

You don't have to explain yourself. I've found this causes more problems than it solves, but if you're setting a boundary with someone close to you it might be helpful to explain where you're coming from if you feel called.

And of course the length of discussion will vary depending on your relationship with the person and the type of issue at hand.

We'll talk more about the difference between being kind and being nice soon. For now, just think about how to state your stance clearly and kindly, taking personal responsibility for your position. If you're feeling guilty in the moment, it helps to get really clear on why this is important to you and what will happen if you DON'T set this boundary.

Step 4. Honor any guilt you feel, but trust the process.

Honoring your true desires is important. Try not to allow guilt to influence your actions.

Guilt related to boundary setting typically comes from feeling unworthy, like your preferences matter less than another person's.

Guilt can also come from shame, and feeling like speaking your truth or setting expectations makes you unworthy of love.

Honor this guilt, but don't act from it. Anger and resentment are much more useful guides when it comes to setting boundaries.

If you do lash out or act in a way that you find inappropriate, forgive yourself. But don't allow that feeling to cause you to backtrack from a heartfelt decision that supports your highest self.

You're re-patterning responses. Over time, as you set firm boundaries and become more clear in what's okay, your sense of personal power will grow.

This internal power will help you receive requests and consider them neutrally, without an immediate emotional response. A lot of times anger is the soul's cry for boundaries while the ego, afraid of losing love, feels like it has no choice but to acquiesce to outside expectation.

Empowered in your truth, you'll soon set boundaries in the moment, speaking up for yourself from a place of firmness whenever something doesn't feel good.

The stronger you are in your boundaries and the more effortlessly you communicate your true needs, the less others will respond negatively.

Negative outer responses tend to come when you first set boundaries. If someone is used to you responding in certain ways, it will come as a surprise when you say no or ask to stop being treated that way. They may express anger, but that only reflects their feeling that they have power over you. When you reclaim your power, the other may feel powerless (if they derived their power from feeling they had control over you) and lash out.

Keep your cool and know that how we respond speaks about our internal world and how the other responds speaks to their internal world. The more certain you are in who you are, others will sense that certainty and will challenge you less.

Journal prompts:

How did your parents handle boundaries and speaking about their needs? How does that influence you? Did your parents easily express their needs or did they wait until they were angry or overwhelmed? What do you tend to do?

What messages have you taken on from the world about how you must show up for others? How does that make you feel?

What areas in your life need better boundaries? Where do you feel overwhelmed? What do you constantly complain about? What boundaries do you need to set around those areas?

What fears do you have around setting boundaries? How can you see that differently? What will happen if you don't set boundaries? Feel free to invoke your higher self or ask the universe for insight.

_____
_____
_____
_____
_____
_____
_____
_____
_____
_____
_____
_____
_____
_____
_____
_____
_____
_____
_____
_____
_____
_____
_____
_____
_____
_____
_____
_____
_____
_____

_____
_____
_____
_____
_____
_____
_____
_____
_____
_____
_____
_____
_____
_____
_____
_____
_____
_____
_____
_____
_____
_____
_____
_____
_____
_____
_____

Day 18: Nice or kind?

This week as we're exploring self-expression and ways of reclaiming lost pieces of yourself, it's important to consider the difference between being nice and being kind.

A lot of times these words are used interchangeably, but they're actually two very different things. Understanding this difference will help you set boundaries and say no in a way that feels good to you. It'll also help you identify other areas of life where you're giving your power away for the sake of being liked.

What's the difference between being nice and being kind?

Being nice tends to come from a feeling of unworthiness rather than a sincere desire to show compassion.

Niceness tends to be more about trying to win another person's love or affection, and fearing that if you're not nice, you'll be ostracized. It's people pleasing.

At worst, it's the classic act of pasting a smile on your face all while you're seething inside. Nice favors social acceptability more than speaking your truth.

I'm not saying there's never a place to be nice, but it's important to understand the distinction between niceness and kindness so you can make an educated decision.

Choosing niceness over your truth injures your soul. It essentially says that how you really think and feel isn't okay. That saying no to a request or allowing yourself to be walked on is a requirement for you to receive love.

Being kind, on the other hand, is rooted in compassion.

Kindness is compassion for yourself and others. It's infusing the expression of what you truly think and feel with the energy of love. Kindness is being assertive without being aggressive, although you can certainly express your feelings if you're feeling angry.

Like we talked about in Day 14, kindness is the ability to stand firm in your energetic boundaries, connect to your heart and voice your truth with love. Kindness comes from a place of generosity, of loving your fellow human as much as you love yourself.

To be kind, simply state how you truly think and feel. If something bothers you, speak up! It's not necessary to apologize for how you think and feel, either. All your thoughts and feelings are valid and worthy of expression.

Kindness is firm. It's rooted in your deeper values.

Niceness has a sense of weakness to it, with undercurrents of a constant plea: *please like me.*

Finding a sense of kindness begins within, with how we treat ourselves. Niceness lets you off the hook easily. *Ugh. I don't want to do this journaling work right now because it just doesn't feel good. I'll eat ice cream instead!* That might feel nice in the moment, but it's not kind. (Not that it's not okay to slack off. It is. But when it becomes a pattern, it becomes a problem.)

Kindness honors what's good for you not just in this moment, but in the long run. It takes strength to be kind. It takes strength to sit with pain. To have uncomfortable conversations. To see things differently. To forgive. To love.

Honor the process.

Today is about becoming aware of this difference. Going forward, become more aware of your communications with self and others, and seek to embody a compassionate kindness that resonates with you.

If you're not used to speaking your truth, your voice may initially be tinged with anger, but that only reflects your inner feelings of powerlessness that your voice won't be taken seriously.

For you, this is a process of personal empowerment, knowing that you are capable of setting boundaries and establishing requirements for how you want to be treated. The more rooted you feel in your desires, the more powerfully and kindly you'll be able to express yourself.

And of course, those who veer toward the softer side of things may need to purposefully rouse that inner fire to release the fear of saying what you truly think and feel. There's that saying, speak your truth even if your voice shakes. Just begin! It'll get easier.

A lot of times under niceness is a sea of anger, left unprocessed from years of allowing yourself to be walked all over. If anger rises up, it's okay. Feel it, honor it, and know where it's coming from so you can work through it and establish new, more empowered ways of communication.

Find your authentic communication style.

As an East Coaster living on the West Coast, I think about this a lot. On the East Coast, everyone is blunt and assertive. I now live on the West Coast and everyone is super laid back. When I first moved out West, I tempered my communication style a lot, but lost a piece of myself.

To this day, sometimes I say things really bluntly and people get offended. It's a constant balance to stay true to myself while still taking other people's feelings into consideration.

Personally, I like when other people are direct with me, but other people may prefer a more gentle approach.

The thing is, you can't make everyone happy. Just because someone dislikes your delivery doesn't make you wrong. The most important thing you can do is be true to you.

The right people will come into your life and the people who don't mesh well will fall away.

Like everything else in life, it's about finding what works for you and what feels good. The more true you are to you, the more specific your self-expression will become.

Maybe more people won't like you. But for every person who doesn't, another loves you that much more. Ultimately, it's better to be hated for who you are than to be loved for a fake version of you. Take off the mask. Love who you are. Be who you are. No matter what.

Journal prompts:

What are your experiences with being nice and being kind? What does your communication style veer toward? What are the reasons for that?

When it comes to speaking your truth, what problems do you experience? Take a moment to connect with your higher self. How could you see those problems differently?

Do you apologize for saying how you think and feel? Why is that? How can you re-pattern this?

How could you treat yourself or talk to yourself more kindly? How could you treat others more kindly? (This may mean shifting out of niceness and into kindness or having more compassion.)

Visualize yourself setting a boundary powerfully and calmly. How would you feel while speaking? What kinds of words would you use? How do you feel afterward?

Consider creating an affirmation for when you speak your truth but someone doesn't react well. It could be something like, "My highest purpose is to speak my truth. I will always consider whether I could have been more kind, but this is my journey and all I can do is to show up the best I can every day."

_____

_____

_____

_____

_____

_____

_____

_____

_____

_____

_____

_____

_____

_____

_____
_____
_____
_____
_____
_____
_____
_____
_____
_____
_____
_____
_____
_____
_____
_____
_____
_____
_____
_____
_____
_____
_____
_____
_____
_____

_____
_____
_____
_____
_____
_____
_____
_____
_____
_____
_____
_____
_____
_____
_____
_____
_____
_____
_____
_____
_____
_____
_____
_____
_____
_____
_____
_____
_____
_____

Day 19: Inner power.

Today's topic is an important one. Where are you giving your power away? Our society has a really messed up relationship with power. We think of having power over another person or deriving power from money or office.

The true source of power is from within. True power comes from connection to the divine, the spirit and your highest self.

Viewed this way, self-love, as the process of developing a relationship with your true self, is also a process of reclaiming your power. Because you're literally connecting to the power within.

Common ways we give our power away

The typical ways we give our power away include asking for permission to do things, needing outside approval to pursue a dream, an opportunity, take a trip, wear an outfit or like a certain thing.

Have you ever waited to decide if you like a movie or a song until seeing what other people around you thought? I used to do this.

I had people in my life I thought were cool, cooler than me apparently, and would wait to see what they thought before I made up my own mind.

Sometimes even something this simple, deciding our opinion before asking what other people think, can be a pathway to reclaiming power.

How to reclaim your power:

We've already talked about boundaries, which are an important part of reclaiming your power, so let's discuss a few other ways to honor the true brilliance of your soul.

Step 1. Honor your emotional experience.

The relationship most people have with their emotions creates a profound sense of disempowerment because it's based on resistance, judgment, fighting and repression rather than love, acceptance, and understanding.

Society tells us to fight our feelings and hide our deepest pains, which is why so many of us feel there's something wrong with us. Pain doesn't make us flawed; it makes us human. Society wants us to fit in boxes and move on from trauma, sickness and loss without skipping a beat. When we feel pain from unprocessed trauma or from struggling to fit in socially approved boxes, we're told there's something wrong with us.

As you honor how you feel rather than how you think you should feel, you are discovering what's real and true for you — and you don't need anyone else to validate what you know in your heart. As you reconnect to your inner power, you find the courage to feel how you feel, live how you want to live, and be who you want to be. Ironically, the more you can open up to your pain, the greater joy and freedom you feel.

Step 2. Keep your own counsel.

Try this: For one week, don't ask anyone for their opinion.

How often do you wait to talk to your mom, dad, sister, and five friends before making a decision? It can be really helpful to just tune in and ask your intuition. (We'll talk more about intuition soon.)

You don't need outside perspectives because your soul knows the exact perfect path to get you where you want to go. Nobody outside of you has access to this knowledge. It can be helpful to talk things over with people, but to know which advice is truly good for you and which will only hurt you, you must be able to run any outside input through your own internal detector.

Recall the first week when we talked about alignment. How does this advice make you feel? Good advice / epiphanies / insights / suggestions will feel light or expansive or grounded. Bad-for-you advice or insights will feel heavy. You might feel frustrated, overwhelmed or annoyed.

You may judge yourself for these feelings, but they're just signs of misalignment. That's why asking for advice isn't a substitute for your own internal guidance system, but more a supplement. Even going through this journal — if something doesn't resonate with you, don't take it on as your own!

I can only share what's worked for me, but this whole process is about finding out what works for you.

Another quick note: Asking others for guidance can be also be the ego's way of playing it safe. Relying on others almost gives you someone to blame if something doesn't work out. To reclaim your power is also to reclaim personal responsibility for your life.

Step 3. Examine where another person's boundaries or expectations have become your own.

Where are you needing outside approval for following your heart? Almost every time I've done something truly spectacular, I've had pushback from those around me who feared for my safety.

A few years ago, I traveled to Costa Rica alone. My husband was so scared I'd get robbed and then shot that his fears became my own. I almost cancelled the trip.

But I didn't. I went, and of course I was cautious the whole time, but the trip was amazing and just what my soul needed.

Another time, also a few years ago, I remember thinking the pathway to my happiness was being the good employee, the good wife. It's like when I got married, I lost myself and took on social expectations of what a wife (and respectable adult) was supposed to be.

One day I felt so frustrated, like I was keeping the house clean, working long hours, doing everything I thought I was expected to do, pleasing everyone but myself. I felt so powerless, like I wasn't receiving the love I desired in exchange for being this respectable person.

I don't remember what the trigger was, but suddenly it became crystal clear how I'd given my power away, tried to fill a role while losing myself in the process.

I let it all go, all the expectations, and began setting my own, asking myself what I wanted and what I expected of myself. Setting my own criteria for worthiness instead of gauging it on my ability to fill this social role that nobody was even asking me to fill. It was all in my head.

Step 4. Find the lesson in whatever you're resisting.

My course The Big Shift goes deeper into accepting your life as it is, but think about whatever situation is causing you the most duress. How can you see it differently? What is life asking of you? How can you rise up? How can you let go?

What expectations of how life should be or how you thought it would turn out are holding you back from following your heart's intuitive guidance?

We can give our power away to people, but also to life circumstances by wishing they were different than they are. Accept all things, and then decide your next steps. You are a warrior.

Journal prompts:

Explore any of the questions peppered throughout today's reading.

Also: Where are you waiting for outside approval before doing something meaningful to you?

Where in your life are you looking outside of yourself for answers? What is the answer you know deep within?

Where are you allowing other people's fears / rules / expectations influence your own? If you could do what you really wanted to do, what would you do?

What roles are you playing? How can you define your own sense of self-worth?

_____
_____
_____

_____
_____
_____
_____
_____
_____
_____
_____
_____
_____
_____
_____
_____
_____
_____
_____
_____
_____
_____
_____
_____
_____
_____
_____
_____
_____
_____
_____
_____
_____

Day 20: Unlock your intuition.

Today is all about intuition. If you've been disconnected from yourself for awhile, this voice may be really quiet. It'll take time to hear your inner wisdom again, but take heart.

As you continue setting the intention and making an effort to connect, you'll soon again be swimming in the flow of divine knowledge to guide your way on.

What is intuition?

Intuition is your connection to your higher self. It's a knowing beyond knowing.

Energetically, it relates to the sixth chakra, which is the third eye, and is supported by the seventh chakra, at the crown of the head, which relates to your divine connection.

Physically, intuition can speak through emotions, a funny feeling or gut instinct. Perhaps a specific image or scene may come to mind.

Thoughts can also be part of the intuitive response. Everyone talks about how evil thoughts are, but inspired guidance often comes in the form of a thought that just won't let go. We often try to convince ourselves differently, rationalize, or find the logic, but it's important to listen to ourselves because deep down, you always know the truth.

It can be hard to tell the difference between ego thoughts and those fueled by spirit, but over time you'll understand the difference. It's a process of tuning in, taking the guidance, and then reflecting on whether that was in fact the right decision.

This reflection is essentially tuning your intuition like an instrument. With practice, over time, you'll know all the right chords.

What is the difference between fear and intuition?

In my experience, if something is meant for you, there will be a current of desire beneath the fear. In warning-sign fear, there's no desire. It's almost as if your whole body tenses up against the unknown.

What about when intuition leads to a seemingly wrong decision?

I don't believe this happens. Looking back, each time I've made an unfortunate choice based on what I thought was my intuition, there were always red flags. I ignored these signs or my inner knowing, instead paying attention to my ego needs and desires of how I thought things should work out. And it backfired.

That said, there are ultimately no wrong decisions, only those made at different levels of consciousness.

Sometimes a seemingly bad situation leads us where we're meant to be. Other times, maybe our soul needed to learn something and although the lesson is painful, it's still where we're meant to be. If we hadn't needed to learn that lesson, we would have chosen differently. We're always doing the best we can.

I know that's not an easy thing to swallow, but life is a school and unfortunately, humans tend to learn through pain. The key is to embrace and accept the present moment and keep moving forward the best you can.

How to strengthen your intuition:

Step 1. Have a strong spiritual practice.

This is probably the most important way to strengthen your intuition. A spiritual practice not only creates space in your body, mind and heart to receive inspired guidance, but it also deepens your connection to the spiritual world, ensuring you receive more guidance.

Meditation in particular is a wonderful way to strengthen your intuition.

Step 2. Listen to it.

This may seem obvious, but how many times have you asked for an answer or sign and then not followed the guidance when it came? Intuition speaks to us all day long, telling us to take a break or read a certain book or eat a certain food.

By not listening, we're essentially telling this guidance that we don't want it. The universe is based on free will. Guidance is always readily available to us, but we have to first ask and second, show that we want it. If a friend kept asking you to dinner, but you said no every time, I bet that friend would give up pretty soon!

When connecting with your intuition, it's important to go with that first flash of insight. Try not to overthink it because overthinking leads to doubt. The thing about intuition, is that it's something you've always known. It comes from the eternal.

Step 3. Ask for help with small things.

You can ask for guidance about what to wear that day, what to eat, which book to read next, or for any number of things.

Each day, I ask my intuition what to wear and an image always comes to mind. It's funny because sometimes I go against that image and try on another outfit, but it never fails — I always end up trying on five different things before ultimately replicating the image in my mind.

It's pretty cool to imagine something and bring it to life, even if it's just an outfit. Small things lead to big things, right?

At this point, I receive images of my next steps all day long. Sometimes I follow them and other times I think my small self knows better, but life is always better when guided by that deeper knowing.

I mention that to underscore the idea that if you open yourself up to receive guidance and follow it, you'll soon receive more. Then, you'll be well connected to this guidance when it comes to the really important things in life.

And actually the small things are important because they create beautiful moments. If life is a series of moments strung together, having more beautiful moments means having a more beautiful life.

Step 4. Trust it.

This week's inquiry has been all about reclaiming your power, and intuition is perhaps one of the biggest pieces to that. To trust your knowing, your insights, your desires and yourself.

To not waffle in over-thinking, but instead tune in, connect to your truth at that moment, and move forward based on how you feel. This is about true power, not the kind that involves muscling your way through life, but instead the power that comes from being connected to something deep within.

Following your intuition to create your life is all about taking small steps forward. You might not know where you're going, but the soul asks you to trust and follow its lead.

Your higher self loves you and is always guiding your path forward. The guidance of your true self is always there. It's just a matter of getting quiet and tuning in.

Journal prompts:

Here's a great exercise called automatic writing.

Take a few moments in silence to connect to your heart and the stillness within.

Write down a sentence about something that's troubling you. And then begin writing. Without thinking. Don't worry if it makes sense. Just write whatever comes to mind.

I've had crazy experiences of connecting to my dead relatives, higher self, whoever. Just open yourself up to the experience and let it flow through you. Don't judge it.

Judgment and fear will close off your intuition. It's like learning to ride a bike — the second you realize you're balanced, you freak out and fall off. So just know that and allow yourself to really just sink in and go with the flow.

———————————————————————————
———————————————————————————
———————————————————————————
———————————————————————————

_____

_____

_____

_____

_____

_____

_____

_____

_____

_____

_____

_____

_____

_____

_____

_____

_____

_____

_____

_____

_____

_____

_____

_____

_____

_____

Day 21: Raise your voice to open your heart.

Today I'm offering you a truly beautiful practice! The chance to sing and open your heart.

Spiritually, singing is best known for opening the throat chakra, the center of speaking your truth. But singing also opens the heart, particularly when you spend time with beautiful songs like the one you'll have the option to sing today.

In yoga, there's a practice known as kirtan which is essentially call and response chanting / singing. It's set to music and is designed to quiet the mind through the repetitive chanting of mantras.

Spending a few moments chanting makes it easier to sink into splendid silence afterward.

Today's practice is not so much chanting, but a beautiful song created from a Kundalini prayer. I first experienced it at a full moon kundalini class, and the feelings of bliss and love that filled my body afterward felt so good.

Singing this way shows devotion to the universe, your higher self, or whatever you believe in.

The path of love is the path of devotion.

Your daily spiritual practice of yoga, meditation or journaling is ultimately inspired by devotion. Devotion to what you know is possible, devotion to give yourself the peace and happiness you know you deserve, devotion to the universe for giving you the gift of life and infinite possibility.

Those times in my life when I feel the most happy and at peace are also those times when I spend most of my time thinking about God / the universe / the infinite / the big picture.

That's what taking a few moments to sing does. It tunes you in. And as a benefit, today you get to absorb the beautiful, gracious spirit of Snatam Kaur, whose voice will guide you through this special song.

Even if this is out of your comfort zone, I encourage you to give it a try! Sing in your car if you're nervous to belt it out at home!

But with this song or another, opening your throat and heart through singing is a beautiful way to connect to the sacred, allow it to infuse your life, uplift you and help you remember all the beauty that surrounds you.

May this practice leave you feeling at peace and full of hope. As long as you have yourself, you have the world.

Our song for today is...

May The Long Time Sun Shine Upon You, a Kundalini farewell mantra sung by Snatam Kaur, a kundalini-inspired musician.

The song includes the mantra "sat nam," which is a Kundalini mantra that means *truth is my name.*

Sat nam recognizes the oneness of all humanity and honors our place in that oneness. Chanting sat nam pulls heavenly energy down into your body, filling you up with the light of awareness.

For those who don't know, Kundalini is a type of yoga that's designed to raise kundalini energy, which is said to lie coiled at the base of the spine, up along the spine toward the crown chakra.

The song is four minutes. Four little minutes to try something out of your comfort zone and could leave you feeling full of bliss and love!

Try this...

Find the song on YouTube or Spotify. Sing the song sitting cross-legged, perhaps on the edge of a pillow for support, and place your hands over your heart.

Give it a try and then let me know how it goes for you!

Journal prompts:

What are you devoted to? What is your highest vision for yourself, your dream of what you know is possible?

_____
_____
_____
_____
_____
_____
_____
_____
_____
_____
_____

_____
_____
_____
_____
_____
_____
_____
_____
_____
_____
_____
_____
_____
_____
_____
_____
_____
_____
_____
_____
_____
_____
_____
_____
_____
_____
_____
_____
_____
_____
_____

Week 4: Rediscovering your dreams

This week is all about connecting to your true desires, finding the flow and allowing yourself to receive.

You'll learn how to create from deep within, so you'll avoid common self-worth traps leading to workaholism and burnout.

Day 22: What do you desire?

This week is all about reclaiming your dreams. And what better way to kick this discussion off than talking about desire?

My relationship with desire has evolved a lot over the past few years. I began a journey of surrender because of unrequited desire. A desire to live somewhere other than I did, do something other than I was, feel another way than I felt.

I surrendered and found great peace. For a little while, I flowed through life not so much desire-less, but I had let go of a previous life vision and a new one had not yet fully formed. The vision was too vague to create desire.

Then time went on, my vision clarified, and desire intensified.

I fell into workaholism trying to realize these desires on my timeline, driven by the idea that if I only worked harder, I could realize my dreams in less time.

From one extreme to another.

Now, I'm developing a healthier relationship with desire.

I take great joy in uncovering the yearnings of my heart, and for the first time in my life, truly believing anything is possible.

I'm also learning to find joy in the space between desire and the present moment. To understand that the beauty of life is in the journey and not the arriving.

Because the second we arrive, we only want to go someplace else. One goal achieved, and another one immediately gets set. That's just how it is.

I've had the good fortune of achieving many big goals in my life, and each one feels very anti-climactic. I wake up the next day the same person inside. New problems inevitably arise to replace old ones.

The outside does affect the inside. I moved, and that made me happy. I'm pursuing a passion, and that makes me happy. But the inside comes first. You can leave a horrible job and still hate life. You can move to a cool new city and still be miserable.

Ultimately, it's all about how you feel inside. Living in such a way that creates the feeling of what you desire, and then allowing whatever is meant for you to flow to you. Letting go and trusting that everything is working out in your favor.

It's all about the journey, anyway. In life we alternate between seasons, or even moments, of surrender and letting go, followed by more active phases of crystallizing our desires and actualizing our plans.

Sometimes you're defining and other other times you're exploring. It's all about tuning in and honoring where you are in this phase of life, and just going with the flow.

Explore this journey from a sense of wholeness, knowing that we don't need anything outside of us. But also acknowledging that pursuing meaningful goals enriches our lives.

Transform needy clinging into a joyful pursuit.

It helps to hold on loosely to the things we want. To set the intention of receiving what you desire, but then letting go.

The tighter we hold on, it seems the further our goals run away. Adopting a sense of play, pursuing goals and desires with a sense of joyfulness that comes from self-expression — that's an approach that allows us to follow our dreams while enjoying the process.

Part of the problem with desire is that it naturally causes separation between you, the present moment, and this thing you want but don't have. This space can inspire you or ruin you.

To let it inspire you, stay grateful for what you have, while wanting more. It's a tricky balance. One that requires practice, but it's essential. Because desire is human nature. We're literally borne of desire. To be a passionate, alive being is to allow the joy of pursuing your dreams, goals and desires light you up from within.

That's okay. Just don't make your desires more important than your happiness. Never forget that you want this thing so you can be happy. You can be happy now — without the thing.

Know that you already have inside of you everything you need. Everything already exists; it's just a matter of welcoming it in. Creating space and being the person who would inevitably receive it.

Create a relationship with your goals and desires.

Allow them to speak to you. The best goals and desires come from deep within.

Because desires, at best, are nudges from your soul, which knows clearly the potentials and possibilities for your life and is always guiding you toward the fullest possible self-expression. Realizing these goals will require you to evolve into the person you're meant to be. Each next stop along the path will ask something of you. To let go, to try something new, to face a fear.

Each step matters, no matter how seemingly small. So write your desires down. Sit with them. What do they want from you?

For example, I want to help millions of people discover themselves through the sacred art of journaling. I want to help people love and understand themselves, to create lives as unique as they are. To inspire people to trust themselves and follow their hearts to realize their dreams.

I want to travel the world and be supported by a successful online business that allows me the freedom to live wherever I feel called. I want to attend spiritual retreats and learn from masters to deepen my own journey of healing and growth so I can pass these tools on to others.

Each step forward requires evolving in new ways, overcoming fear, embodying more confidence and releasing cares of what other people think. More deeply. All the time.

My desires have required me to learn new skills. I've taken courses and hired mentors, read books, faced my fears and navigated deep uncertainty using only my intuition. I've learned to believe. By sitting with your desire, creating space to listen to it, it will communicate with you.

You'll be guided to each right next step. Your intuition will speak and then, just like when you purchased this journal, you'll know it's time to act.

The caveat to all this evolution is...

It can lead you right back where you started, trying to fix yourself in the misbelief that there's something wrong with you and that's why you're not getting what you want.

Stay connected to yourself, prioritize your spiritual practice, and it will flow. You'll mess up, but you'll figure it out.

When I stay connected to my true self, the more patience I have, realizing that each moment matters. Even if my vision is not yet fully realized, this moment has beauty, and one day I'll look back and crave the simplicity of today just like right now I look back in awe at the simplicity of the very start.

Each step of the journey has something special to offer. The more we can sink in and appreciate that while staying connected to our desires, the more we can move forward fueled by desire while dwelling in a place of peace and wholeness.

Believing in possibility makes anything possible.

Let life flow through you. Ask yourself what you want and take the time to truly listen. Let your heart guide you to the life you're meant for. Even if it's not the one your mind thought you should have.

Journal prompts:

What do you desire? Let your pen flow. Write about how you want to feel emotionally and in your body, where you want to live, what kinds of relationships you'd like to have, how you want to feel supported, what kind of work you want to do, what kind of money you want to make, and how you want to feel as you move through the world.

If at any time you get stuck, write, "If I did know what I wanted, what would I want?" You do know! This is a great opportunity to find out.

Look down your list. Write any beliefs about why something isn't possible for you. Is that ultimately true? Notice any feelings of guilt, brattiness or impossibility that come up. Feel free to dig into them, asking why you feel that way.

To balance it out, you might also write a list of things you're grateful for. Writing a list of desires and gratitudes each morning is a beautiful practice.

_____
_____
_____
_____
_____
_____
_____
_____
_____
_____
_____
_____
_____
_____
_____
_____
_____
_____
_____
_____
_____
_____
_____
_____
_____
_____
_____
_____
_____
_____

Day 23: What's your life purpose?

Every single one of us has a unique soul purpose. Many people think of purpose as something you do, but the purpose of your life is to be who you are.

This certainly involves doing things and giving your truest gifts to the world. However it also involves learning the lessons your soul is here to learn, which are a continuum from past life experiences.

Learning these lessons helps you be more authentically you because the entire reason people act inauthentically, or out of alignment with who they really are, stems from a place of acting to get unconscious needs met rather than acting from a place of wholeness.

The human journey involves becoming aware of the ways we've been hurt and finding within us the strength to be present with our pain. This acceptance creates unconditional love from within, which we can then express to the world however we feel called. What you do matters less than the energy you bring to it.

The way each person expresses their love will be so different. Some people are spiritual teachers or healers, but others are makeup artists or actresses or bankers or work at supermarkets. The important thing with purpose is not what you do, but this idea of spreading joy through the act of creation.

The truth about life purpose.

Ultimately the purpose of life is to be the unique person you were born to be. This is why self-love matters. You've got to love yourself to love your expression of self, which is the essence of purpose related to work. The same is true for love, to use an analogy. If you don't love who you are, you won't love the exact match to who you are.

Everyone wants life purpose to be something they do externally, but finding your purpose is more about finding yourself. The task at hand is to be yourself naturally, and trust the flow of your life. The harder you try to figure things out, the more confusing they become. The more you try to figure out how to be you, the further you stray from authenticity.

Humans tend to believe thinking things through erases confusion, but over-thinking intensifies uncertainty. The most important things in life can't be thought through, but felt as true deep within the heart.

Confusion is an energy. It's ultimately the energy of fear — even a fear as simple as fearing you don't know the answer. To find clarity, go within. Connect to yourself. Spend time meditating. Practicing yoga. Hiking. Just being.

This clear connection to your soul creates clarity, and from this place you will receive inspiration for next steps. Your job is to follow your inspiration and curiosity, going wherever it leads. Follow this impulse with all your heart trusting it will take you where you're meant to go. If you'd like more support with this, check out Soul Scroll's Listen to Your Heart guided journal.

The more you can erase doubt, fear and worry, and simply express yourself in the world as you feel called to, the more easily you will find your perfect place in the world.

It's of course wonderful to set goals and intentions, but it's important to make sure these goals and intentions are based upon a true, heartfelt desire rather than because you think achieving a goal will give you status or money, help you fit in, be good enough or impress other people.

There's nothing inherently wrong with these things, but anything achieved at the expense of the soul costs too much. Growing in pursuit of your goals is a good thing. Sacrificing the core of who you are, which brings along a sense that something isn't right, is never worth it. Even if you achieve the goal, you'll be unhappy and which you had chosen differently.

Your true life path and purpose is found by first finding peace and happiness within, and from this place of divine contentment, allowing your inspiration to guide you forward.

Of course you will experience fear, doubt and tribulation — that's just life — but even in those moments you can find love. You can give yourself grace and keep moving forward the best way you know how.

It's very important to value your connection to self over any external purpose, which can become a search for external validation.

Even our goals aren't really about the goal, but about who we become on the way to achieving it. This can be a helpful litmus test to see if something is worth continuing. Always ask yourself, "do I like the person I'm becoming?" If the answer is no, then it's time to shift.

Defining yourself by any external thing is dangerous because it's easy to start believing the external thing is your reason for being. In this unfortunate case, who you are becomes an extension of what you DO rather than allowing who you ARE to come first.

Another reason defining yourself by something outside can backfire is that your purpose will evolve. You may be called to release one iteration of something that felt purposeful and move onto something else. If you define yourself by some role you're playing, you won't allow yourself to evolve, and what once felt purposeful and expansive will end up feeling limiting and suffocating.

Also, worldly things involve moving through disappointment and failure. If you gauge your worth externally, this measure will constantly fluctuate based on how well you're meeting your goals. It's got to be deeper. Your sense of self-worth must be derived from your connection to self and the universe, or however you choose to define what makes you valuable.

The truth is, you can release something totally heartfelt in the world and hear crickets or criticism. It's deeply painful, but it's all part of the journey. It doesn't mean you're on the wrong path. The way to know if you're on the right path is by how you feel.

You already have everything you need to make your dreams come true.

Even if you think you don't. I remember wanting to be a literary non-fiction writer so badly and thinking I had messed up my entire life by becoming a small town newspaper reporter and then moving to Arizona, which is not shall we say the literary capital of the world.

But life refused to give up on me. My intuition kept telling me the next steps to take. My heart kept telling me to stop resisting and accept everything. Because once I accepted the things I didn't like, I found the spaces between. In space, there is possibility. Even though some steps didn't go anywhere, they mattered.

Quit your job and go freelance, my heart whispered. Stop writing for online marketers and get your name in magazines. It was only after realizing an early dream — seeing an article I wrote on the cover of a magazine — that I realized this dream was no longer mine. I felt nothing.

It was time to start over. Time to ask the questions. What next? Why am I here? Maybe it was okay that I was in Arizona, after all. Maybe I was exactly where I was supposed to be. My heart began whispering. Start a blog. Create a course. Eventually that path ended, and I felt stuck again. I had to let things go and find clarity and peace within once more. From this place of peace, the process began again.

I never in a million years could have guessed this would all come together the way it did. But it did. Even though I thought I was lost in a place, I was actually exactly where I was supposed to be for all my dreams to unfold. We're always exactly where we're supposed to be, from the perspective that where we are is perfect for our soul's expansion and expression.

Even if you feel like you messed up, it's all perfect from the soul's perspective in that there were some things you needed to learn. Forgive yourself. It's okay. Receive the wisdom and begin again. There's always a right next step. Always a way to surrender more deeply to what is and what your heart is asking for. All you have to do is ask for guidance and be brave enough to listen.

Journal prompts:

What makes you unique? How do you love to express yourself? If you're not sure, what feels like something cool you feel called to learn about or create? What curiosities do you have?

Where are you not expressing yourself fully? How could you express yourself a little more? What projects have been hinting in your mind that you'd like to move forward with?

How is how you thought life would turn out limiting you from taking advantage of the opportunities in front of you? What opportunities are in front of you that you're not taking advantage of? If you feel like you're waiting for something, what is that about?

How would you show up in the world if you were living in a way that wholly reflected your true self?

_____
_____
_____
_____
_____
_____
_____
_____
_____
_____
_____
_____
_____
_____
_____
_____
_____
_____
_____
_____
_____
_____
_____
_____
_____
_____
_____
_____
_____

_____
_____
_____
_____
_____
_____
_____
_____
_____
_____
_____
_____
_____
_____
_____
_____
_____
_____
_____
_____
_____
_____
_____
_____
_____
_____

Day 24: Perfectionism and true confidence.

Tomorrow we're going to start turning your dreams into plans, but first I want to help you get over yourself.... in the nicest possible way!

Untapped potential will destroy you. You were born to express yourself. You'll find healing in the self-expression. Don't wait. Begin today.

You might be waiting to be more confident, have more money, to be more perfect or talented, or for a better time, but the truth is that the time to begin is now.

Confidence comes from knowing who you are and walking your unique path through life with love, not fear.

A lot of times you might wait to feel confident before you try something new, but the truth is you'll be waiting forever. If you have a dream, or want to try something new, do it now.

The times in my life I felt the most unstoppable were those times that I wanted to give up because it felt like my dreams were crashing all around me, but I dug my heels in and kept going anyway.

This is why self-love comes before following your dreams even though it's easy to think achieving a dream will make you happy. It's so important to connect to a sense of love and validation from within because the world will test you. The world is not a place to receive assurances and validation. The world is where you give the things you've created from within. The manifestation of a dream may make you temporarily happy, but trials come. Losses happen. The way to pick yourself up and rise up again is by connecting to yourself and loving yourself unconditionally. Keep going because giving up would be giving up on yourself. Every failure is just a stepping stone to success.

Let repetition be your effort.

We have these fully formed images of ourselves and wait until we believe we're capable of producing this level of greatness before putting ourselves out into the world. The truth is, you'll never get better unless you begin!

Putting things out into the world is really important. There's a certain alchemy that happens from offering your ideas. Seeing how people respond, seeing how it feels once others' eyes are on it — it's an important part of the process. This is important: there is no perfect thing, only an infinitely unfolding process of becoming.

Or maybe you're waiting to have all the answers before making a change in your life. Maybe your perfectionism comes from needing to do endless hours of research instead of trusting yourself that you'll be able to figure it out. It's time to trust yourself. Trust that even if you mess up and fall on your face, you can still love yourself and find your self-worth in the trying, and not in the perfect execution.

Things come to you when you need them.

In life, people sometimes wait to act before having all the pieces laid out before them, which leaves them stuck. One of my favorite quotes is by Martin Luther King Jr. He said, "You don't have to see the whole staircase. Just take the first step." You can't know exactly how it will all turn out, but you'll never find out without taking the next right step.

Living is an art, and whether you're creating a painting, writing a book or building a business, the journey is about receiving things just in time. The more we can trust that we'll receive things as we need them, the more soulful and impactful our creations — and our lives — become.

That's also why you don't need a fully formed idea to begin. Just take the next step. That's all you have to do. Keep taking steps forward. It's all about the continual, 1% improvement, and not needing to deliver a masterpiece before taking Painting 101.

Perfectionism isn't the desire to be perfect.

Perfect doesn't exist. Perfectionism is the desire to prove your worth by being faultless. It's a fear that you're not good enough and therefore nothing you do is good enough.

Our creative efforts are expressions of our souls and everything you do is good enough because inherently, you are good enough.

The trouble with perfectionism is that it stops you from greatness because it stops you from trying. It keeps you in a cycle of trying to prove your ability rather than develop it.

To get good at something, you have to deal with the pain of releasing work in the world that you know could be better. Whether you're writing or teaching yoga or playing music or even in a corporate job somewhere, we're all showing up every day the best way we can.

We get good at things by continuing to show up, by sitting with the discomfort of falling short of your vision, but allowing that vision to inspire you anyway. Dedicate yourself to your effort, and allow repetition to move you forward.

Overcome perfectionism with gratitude.

One of my favorite mantras to overcome perfectionism is, "I'm grateful for my gifts. I value my contributions."

Not releasing your gifts into the world from fear is a really selfish thing to do. You're doing the world a disservice and blocking the full expression of the universe by blocking your own potential.

You can't let fear stop you from releasing all you have to give to the world. You don't have to spend the next five years researching your options. Begin today. You'll figure it out.

Know what vision in your heart is ripe for this time.

It's a balance between starting before you're ready and going too far, too soon.

You've got to plant seeds, and pick the fruits when they're ripe. Wait too long, and the fruit falls to the ground, rotten. But pick too soon, and your first bite is less than juicy. You'll know the truth by how it feels. Is there desire underneath the fear? Or just pure, abject fear? All that's required is to take the right next step.

For example, a lot of people quit their jobs before their dream is ready to sustain them and ultimately return to the 9 to 5. But, sometimes people overstay their welcome at the 9 to 5 and the job kicks them out to unleash the fullness of their vision! (It happened to me!)

The other side to this is to make sure you plant seeds! It's easy to feel frustrated like nothing is happening. But if that's the case, ask yourself — how many seeds have you planted? A saying I heard once wisely stated, Don't look for fruits of seeds you haven't planted.

Keep going even when you feel like you're failing or when it feels like nothing is happening. Keep taking action, learning and improving in everything you do. The process is important. It's the journey of becoming who you really are. Hold the vision and stay inspired by desire while rooting in gratitude.

And above all, believe. Believe in yourself, your vision, your truth and know that with patience, persistence, faith and hope, all things are possible.

Journal prompts:

What do you think needs to be in place before you follow your dreams? What's stopping you from following the whisper in your heart? Is that a real or imagined obstacle? How can you get around it?

What messages do you have from growing up, or maybe during other times in your life, about failure and trying new things? Are those beliefs you want to take on? If not, what new beliefs would you like to adopt?

What is your relationship with perfectionism? Can you give yourself permission to be imperfect?

What thoughts or beliefs would help you feel more confident. Feel free to create an affirmation for yourself to repeat throughout the day.

What seeds for your dreams would you like to plant now?

If you have a clear image of your dreams, envision the version of you living those dreams. What messages does this future you have? What do you need to know to move forward?

_____
_____
_____
_____
_____
_____
_____
_____
_____
_____
_____
_____
_____
_____
_____
_____
_____
_____
_____
_____
_____
_____
_____
_____
_____
_____
_____
_____
_____
_____

_____

_____

_____

_____

_____

_____

_____

_____

_____

_____

_____

_____

_____

_____

_____

_____

_____

_____

_____

_____

_____

_____

_____

_____

_____

_____

_____

_____

Day 25: Make it a habit.

Today I have a delicious question for you — how can you live in a way that honors your true goals, desires, values and dreams? How can you live in a way that makes you feel loved or wanted or abundant or successful?

It all comes down to habit. You are what you do daily.

What new habits you create will depend on where you are on your journey.

If you're ready to follow your dreams, pick one thing that will get you closer to that, even if that's practicing your skills or promoting yourself on social media or making phone calls.

Maybe you're feeling directionless in life. If so, maybe spend 10 minutes a day meditating or journaling or walking in nature, connecting to your higher self until a message comes through about your next steps, some way you can shift to feel more expansive.

Maybe you want more magic in your life and would love to do something like watch the sunset each night. Soak in the feeling that anything is possible.

Today is also an invitation to examine your existing habits and identify which serve you and which don't.

These could be internal habits, like complaining or criticizing yourself or others, or external, like eating unhealthy food or watching too much television.

If you're not sure what your habits are, start the inquiry there. Every few hours, set a reminder on your phone to check in, see what you're doing and how it makes you feel. Our lives are literally a collection of habits. If you change your habits, you'll change your life. This can feel overwhelming, so I have tips for you!

The best way to create a new habit:

Rather than overhaul your life, it helps to focus on creating one new habit at a time. Focus on micro-shifts. Small changes add up over time.

It can be good to choose what I call a linchpin habit, something that influences everything else in your life. For example, if you're not sleeping enough, and ultimately wake up late, skip breakfast and run out of the house feeling like a mess, then getting more sleep would help your whole life feel better. This also illustrates why, for example, setting the goal of creating a morning ritual might not work until addressing the issue of sleep.

Once you've decided on the new habit you want to create, here are my tips for creating the new habit:

Step 1. Connect to your why.

Why do you want to create this habit? Knowing why will help you overcome the inevitable resistance linked to change. Just ask yourself, why does it matter?

Maybe you want to exercise to feel good, reduce stress, improve your mood and boost your energy levels. You want to look good in your clothes and feel more confident.

Maybe deeper, you're worried about your health and want to be around for your kids. Go deep and keep asking why until you hit an answer that deeply resonates.

Or maybe you want to face your fears and follow a long-held dream. Why does that matter? Maybe you're tired of spending so many years waiting for the right time.

Maybe you're sure you have great gifts the world needs and that would make you happy to express them, and you're tired of holding yourself back. Maybe truly, you're afraid of dying with your gifts still inside of you. Whatever your why is, this step is really important.

Step 2. For bad habits, why does it serve you? Why do you WANT to keep doing it? How else can you meet that need?

Each bad habit protects us in some way. For example, I used to struggle a lot with going to bed at a decent time. I'd wake up tired and unable to take on the day like I wanted to.

After much inner work, I realized I was subconsciously sabotaging myself from following my dreams. It took time to first realize this, and then to fully understand why this was happening.

Rather than one big epiphany, it was like multiple mini-epiphanies over time. But eventually, I unpacked the reasons for self-sabotage enough to undo the habit. Then, I became very clear why it was important to wake up early and feel energized so I could chase my dreams.

It did take a long time, maybe more than a year,' but just now writing this I realized that I now go to bed early more often than not. Victory! Keep doing the inner work and you'll find your way.

Step 3. Plan how you'll overcome obstacles.

For example, if you want to meditate but always tell yourself you don't need to or don't have time, how can you dismantle that obstacle?

What will you tell yourself instead? How can you create an extra five minutes in the morning? (Taking something away to create space always helps.)

If you want to exercise after work, but find yourself hungry and just go home instead, plan for that. Bring a snack. In the moment when you're resisting, it can help to think of your why. Let your why inspire you past the struggle of creating a new habit.

Step 4. Think about how breaking your promise to yourself affects you.

Once you're mindful and noticing the impulse, it helps to imagine the outcome of the habit you want to drop or create.

Whenever the temptation to stay up late arises, I think of how tired I'll be in the morning and how frustrated that will make me. I have a mantra: Staying up late tonight steals tomorrow's joy. Linking my in-the-moment actions to whatever result I want to create or avoid keeps me on track.

Step 5. Spend your time in valuable ways so the things that don't bring you value have no room in your life.

If you're trying to STOP doing something, it helps to have something else to fill the hole of what you used to do.

Trying to stop losing yourself in an internet black hole? What do you want to do instead? Maybe you want to read a book or work on a hobby. Set the goal of doing that every day, filling your time with things that bring you joy, and soon there will be no space for the things that don't add value to your life.

Step 6. Celebrate the small wins.

When I was working to reduce my internet consumption at night and read instead, some nights I would literally spend 10 fewer minutes online, reading instead.

But instead of criticizing myself for that, I congratulated myself and noticed how good it felt to read instead of get sucked into Facebook or Instagram. That small positive feeling created more momentum, and over time I've been able to spend all my free time in ways that feel better.

We're much more likely to create change by cheering ourselves on instead of whipping ourselves into shape. Sometimes it is necessary to activate your inner parent and be firm with yourself, but it's always from a place of love.

Changing habits isn't about being worthy or good enough, but creating a life you love because you're worth it! If you'd like support with changing your habits, check out our Play with the Day yearly goal journal, which features a years' worth of habit trackers along with support to set monthly goals and intentions. Habit tracking is a powerful way to make new habits stick.

Journal prompts:

What habits would make you feel loved, fulfilled or happy from the inside out? Thinking back to your values and desires, are there any habits that would make your life reflect that deep inner vision?

Make a list of habits you have and examine how they affect your life and make you feel.

Thinking of your bad habits, how do they serve you?

Choose one habit you'd like to make or break and go through the steps listed in today's reading.

_____

_____

_____

_____

_____

_____

_____

_____

_____

_____

_____

_____

_____

_____

_____

_____

_____

_____

_____

_____

_____

_____

_____

_____

_____

_____

_____

_____

_____
_____
_____
_____
_____
_____
_____
_____
_____
_____
_____
_____
_____
_____
_____
_____
_____
_____
_____
_____
_____
_____
_____
_____
_____
_____
_____
_____

Day 26: Find your flow.

Today is all about flow! Sometimes when I plug directions into Google maps on my phone, the automated voice says, "You are now on the fastest route."

That's kind of how flow is. The superhighway to your most fulfilling life. Connecting to flow will lead you straight to your passion and purpose, meaning and joy. Ultimately a life of greater ease. A life where you gracefully receive what's meant for you and let the rest pass you by.

What is flow?

One definition of flow is a state of concentration during which your mind is stretched to its limit, which absorbs you fully into the task at hand so much that nothing else exists. This makes flow almost a spiritual experience because it's highly meditative. It's when time, and maybe even awareness of your physical body, disappears because you're so deeply connected to whatever you're doing.

Dropping into flow connects you to the universe and your higher self, which is the essence of connecting to self-love as we've defined it during this journal.

Another definition of flow is living in the flow of life. Trusting that you're exactly where you're meant to be while opening up to the opportunities for expansion available to you.

Depending upon how much you're used to struggling in life, your threshold for struggle may be very high. The more you drop into flow, the more you realize where you're struggling needlessly, holding on to tension or doing things the difficult way out of habit.

Connecting to flow teaches you a better way through experience. It teaches you how to ride the current of life and respond accordingly, maybe even getting to a point where you slow down or speed up your pace of action depending upon how the energy of your life feels, as if riding a wave.

Struggle versus ease.

When you're in the flow, you're taking action, but it feels like the action comes from stillness, almost like it's bubbling up from within. Time slows down and you're absorbing the energy of the moment and playfully responding, fully connected to both yourself and the universe.

Of course not everything in life is easy, but the more we live from flow, the better it feels. Sometimes we get really stuck on things happening in a specific way, and throw ourselves against brick walls when they aren't working.

Spending time in flow helps us notice when things feel like sludge. That's a sign to take a break, whether for five minutes or five days, to check in with your inner guidance and see if any adjustments are needed.

Sometimes just taking a break brings a fresh perspective. Often those times I feel I absolutely cannot slow down are the times I need it the most.

Flow is a process of surrender and trust. When we flow with the universe, we're harnessing the natural current of what is to arrive at our destination more quickly and pleasurably, feeling supported.

If you're going through a hard time, I don't want to diminish your struggle. Flow is still for you. It's even more important.

Find those moments in time that allow you to forget your problems and feel supported by the universe. Maybe it's a yoga class or watching the sunset. Find what makes you feel connected to the universe and do more of that. Taking time to tune in could very well give you fresh insights to your most troubling problems.

Letting go versus giving up.

If we dedicate ourselves to flow and greater ease, does that mean you give up when it gets hard? What is the difference between letting go and giving up?

These are great questions. First, nothing worthwhile in life is easy, whether that's deepening your relationship with self or others, finding and following your passion, or living a meaningful life. Navigating difficulty is part of the game. It's how we grow strong and develop character.

That said, all of life is a balance, and it's important to balance those times of navigating rocky terrain with finding the sweetness of flow, play and surrender. Letting go is doing the work and letting go of the outcome to enjoy the sweetness of life.

Letting go is a commitment to showing up every day and doing everything you know how to do while trusting the process.

Letting go is releasing your ideas of how you think things should be to embrace how they are, while trusting everything is working out for the highest good.

Sometimes, when something isn't working, it's not a call to give up, but to shift directions. When we let go of our attachment to how things are supposed to be, we are able to hear the inner guidance that allows us to find our way back to feeling good.

Giving up, on the other hand, is releasing all effort and falling into stories about how something isn't possible for you or you don't deserve good things.

Sometimes we do need to quit or dramatically shift directions, but it's important that the energy behind that be of letting go of what's no longer working rather than giving up on a dream because things got hard.

Your commitment makes the difference. We don't always know the answers in life, but if you keep following your heart and trusting that everything will work out, it most certainly will. It has to. Giving up is abandoning the effort and not trying anymore. It's sitting on the couch at home in defeat and staying there, never picking yourself back up to try again.

How to find the flow.

To begin, find one activity that makes you feel free, and spend five minutes a day or maybe an hour a week, fully engaged. Lose yourself in it.

Whether it's meditation or walking or sewing or dancing or running or playing an instrument or even sipping a cup of tea, create little moments of flow throughout your day. The biggest thing is to allow yourself to experiment.

For me, writing creates flow. Although I will say that in between me and the flow were oceans of repressed emotions that manifested as resistance.

So if you're still working through repressed emotions, you may have to clear more space before accessing flow. Or not. Just stay open and see. Maybe flow will help you process.

Flow creates trust.

This is one of the most beautiful parts about finding the flow. Living your life on purpose is very much tied to trust. Trusting yourself and trusting your path through life.

Flow is essentially active surrender. You're literally playing with the universe, tuning in and seeing what comes next.

You might practice yoga on your own without a video or teacher, just tuning into your body and allowing a vision of what pose comes next or feeling of tightness in your body to dictate your next move.

And in following your purpose, it's about tuning in and asking yourself, "What are the next steps?"

This requires trust because you're releasing control. But flow helps create trust. Finding safe places to practice letting go can help you get out of survival mode and surrender.

For example, when I was younger and living in Hawaii, I was healing from deep trauma. I would go into the ocean and throw my body onto the waves. As the waves brought me in, I practiced releasing fully, all tension, and just dropping into the wave.

That was momentary flow, not a long period of time, but it was perfect for then and exactly what I could manage. So flow is about longer times of dropping in, yes, but it's also about finding pockets, safe places where you can practice releasing tension and dropping fully into the present moment.

You could even take a few moments and lie on the floor, allowing your weight to fully drop into the Earth.

The more you release, the more you surrender, the more sweetness you welcome into your life.

Journal prompts:

Where do you struggle the most in life, or where do things feel really hard? What are the stories you tell yourself around these struggles? What meaning do you give to them?

If you were to spend more time pushing your mind or body to its limits to see what you're capable of, what would that look like? (This is from a healthy place rather than pushing yourself to exhaustion or injury.)

How do you navigate the balance between letting go and giving up in your life? Thinking of an area you're struggling with, how do those balances apply? Where do you need to let go? What would you be creating more space for if you did let go?

If you are experiencing the energy of giving up, what are your thoughts and feelings about that? How can you shift?

_____
_____
_____
_____
_____
_____

_____
_____
_____
_____
_____
_____
_____
_____
_____
_____
_____
_____
_____
_____
_____
_____
_____
_____
_____
_____
_____
_____
_____
_____
_____
_____
_____
_____

_____
_____
_____
_____
_____
_____
_____
_____
_____
_____
_____
_____
_____
_____
_____
_____
_____
_____
_____
_____
_____
_____
_____
_____
_____
_____
_____
_____
_____
_____
_____
_____

Day 27: How to receive.

Today's topic could inspire big shifts for you! We're talking about how to receive. We're covering a lot today, but take your time.

If you feel chronically tired, spiritually exhausted, unappreciated, perhaps even resentful, you likely have blocks when it comes to receiving.

A lot of times people who don't know how to receive create relationships with people who don't know how to give. You may not feel worthy of asking for help, ultimately bending over backwards to help people who barely lean forward to meet you.

This results in imbalanced relationships, but because you're not in the habit of receiving, it never occurs to you to create the space to allow your needs to be met.

And if it does occur to you to create this space, it can feel terrifying.

Maybe you fill this space with additional effort, or worries or anything but relaxing and opening up to receive. Or perhaps you anticipate feelings of disappointment before they arrive and react from that feeling, essentially creating the very reality you wanted to avoid.

Of course, sometimes we *are* disappointed by not receiving what we want, whether a goal or support or shift in life. But the difference in reaction between someone who knows their worth and someone who doesn't is very important.

When you know your worth, which is only a matter of deciding, you view disappointment as temporary. It allows you to feel the feelings, but then rebound, objectively evaluate the situation and move forward based on that information.

When you doubt your worth, you take that disappointment as proof that you're flawed or will never get what you want, therefore projecting your temporary feelings of pain and creating an eternally doomed future.

Allowing yourself to receive from the world begins within.

If you do feel chronically unsupported, unheard, unvalidated, the first step is always to tune in and ask — how am I not supporting myself? Listening to myself? Not validating myself? Every outside call is first a call from within.

If you want the world to honor you in specific ways, it's important to first honor yourself. But beyond that, there are few ways you can actively become more receptive.

How to receive:

Step 1. Become comfortable receiving little things.

Gratefully accept compliments when they come your way. Do you explain away your accomplishments or belittle your amazing fashion choices with, *oh? This little thing?*

Own your awesomeness! This is about being so full of yourself that your radiant energy spills over and inspires everyone around you to shine bright like you.

Step 2. Spend time in receptive states.

Receptive states include:

- Gratitude
- Meditating
- Letting go
- Accepting
- Feeling (Receiving all your feelings!)
- Relaxing

Active states include:

- Analyzing
- Doing
- Judging
- Thinking
- Persuading
- Talking

Spending time in receptive states allows you to practice letting go and receiving. Action is the planting of seeds, but then let go and let the universe do her thing.

Step 3. Identify any beliefs making you feel unworthy to receive, or that would block you from receiving.

Free write whatever comes to mind. Common ones include: *Nothing ever works out for me. I never get what I want. Nobody ever helps me. I don't deserve X. That would never happen for someone like me.*

Where did these thoughts come from? Feel those feelings and honor the pain.

Then, see if those beliefs are ultimately true. If they feel true at this moment, how could you shift things so that you move beyond them?

Write a new story. How can you shift your relationship with disappointment or ask for help or show up for yourself in deeper ways so you feel less alone?

4. Stay alert to receptivity blocking.

Now that you're aware, start noticing where you meet people at 80% instead of 50%. Or maybe where people offer help, a beverage, anything, but you say, *oh no, I'm fine.*

A few weeks ago, my husband and I went out to eat and a man in front of me held the door open. I gratefully walked through, but then immediately held the next door open for him! I felt so uncomfortable receiving that I immediately had to return the favor.

Once you become aware, I bet you'll notice all kinds of ways you're blocking receptivity, which is also blocking energy and love. No need to beat yourself up. Just notice and invite a deeper inner shift!

A shadow work process to unroot the pain within blocking your receptivity.

A lot of times unconscious blocks stop us from fully letting go, and it's hard to trust until we unroot them.

Today I offer you a shadow work exercise to help you connect with your inner child and heal any wounds related to receiving. This exercise will help you honor those parts of you who feel neglected or ashamed and stopping you from creating what you want.

Step 1. Get comfortable in a quiet place where you feel safe.

Step 2. Close your eyes and ask to be shown a memory that needs to be healed related to receiving.

Trust whatever image comes to mind. It may seem totally random or unrelated, but trust that the exact perfect memory has come up and has something to tell you.

Step 3. Connect with the vision of you in this memory and start a conversation.

Perhaps you have something to say to the younger you or she has a message to share with you. Notice any of the common core wounds that come up, such as feeling unwanted, a burden, unworthy, rejected, or like an outsider.

Continue this back and forth conversation, feeling free to ask any questions, until you feel a sense of resolution. Be sure to offer words of affirmation and support to the younger version of you.

If you'd like more guidance with this, head to SoulScrollJournals.com/bonuses to access a free shadow work video.

Step 4. Feel any feelings that arise.

Breathe into the sensations. Fully feel them using your breath as a tool to explore the energy. Notice as the emotional energy pulses and moves, eventually dissipating. The bonuses page also includes special access to a 20-minute Feeling Awareness meditation to release emotional pain.

Step 5. Write your observations down. Soak them in.

Repeat this exercise as often as needed. You can adapt this shadow work / inner child healing process to work with any areas of life causing you struggle or frustration. Healing in this way is very powerful.

As you heal the parts of yourself that feel unworthy, you'll allow yourself to receive in deeper ways. It's a lifelong journey. Keep up!

Journal prompts:

Try the shadow work exercise above and then write about your experience.

Other prompts: What is your relationship with receiving? What fears do you have around creating space to receive?

If you have a goal you're working towards right now, how can you find a balance between taking inspired action and then letting go?

_____

_____

_____

_____

_____

_____

_____

_____

_____

_____

_____

_____

_____

_____

_____

_____

_____

_____

_____

_____

_____

_____

_____

_____

_____

_____

_____

_____

_____

_____

_____

Day 28: Fill up on love.

Today is your last self-love practice in the journal before two days of integrating the concepts we've explored over the last month.

It's been a beautiful journey, and today I have a delightful experience for you!

Fill up on love.

Our bodies are instruments of divine understanding, separate entities all on their own, containers for our higher selves and spirit.

Building a relationship to our bodies is an important part of self-love, and one way to nourish that relationship is through conscious eating.

Eating is something all of us do every day, probably every few hours. Maybe you eat with the intention of fueling your body, perhaps you eat to savor the taste of sweetness, maybe you even eat to numb your feelings!

Whatever the case, it's easy to rush through eating, gobbling up to get on with the rest of your day.

Or maybe you notice the hunger and tell yourself that you don't have time to eat just now. Perhaps you've grown accustomed to eating random snacks, overtime transforming your eating into a patchwork of fast fills. Or maybe you binge, trying to satisfy some inner longing.

The problem with this is that food is our connection to Earth, and the way we eat or don't eat says a lot about our relationship with ourselves, how we feel worthy of caring for ourselves, and how worthy we feel of being cared for. Eating is an opportunity to nourish ourselves at the most foundational level.

At best, eating should be a celebration of love and gratitude.

Even the simplest foods can be savored. The sweetness or tartness of a slice of fruit. The satisfying chewiness and raw power contained in protein (if you eat meat). The crunchiness of fresh vegetables, the anti-oxidants and micronutrients absorbed in your body, contributing to your health.

Pausing for a moment of gratitude before a meal can be an amazing way to center in, savor each taste, each mouthful, and acknowledge what a blessing it is to have enough to eat.

Cooking even tastes different when done with love.

There was a time when I viewed eating as something that had to be done, an inconvenience, and not a sacred opportunity to nourish my body, giving me the sustenance to manifest my dreams. I felt eating was an inconvenience because I felt *I* was an inconvenience, that my bodily needs were burdens because deep down, I felt like a burden.

Consciously, this manifested in feeling busy, with no idea what to cook and unwilling to take the time to figure it out. (In fairness, the idea overwhelmed me. My mother was depressed when I was growing up, and for most of my teen years I figured out what to eat alone, filling up on carbs and sweets. There was probably a part of me who was still waiting for someone to feed me and nurture me. Overtime, I've realized I had to do this for myself.) Now an adult, I also felt kind of resentful that I was the only person in my house who made meals. While this is a valid frustration, it was also likely driven by my unhealed inner child, still wishing for someone to cook for her.

And during that time, all of my meals ended up tasting not that wonderful. I'm not an amazing cook, but relatively good, and during that time when I resented cooking, that feeling leaked out into the food and affected the taste of the entire meal.

Now, when I'm cooking, I (try to) view it as a time to nourish and fuel my body, not only with nutrients, but with love.

I actively summon the feeling of love and pour it into the food that I'm cooking. I love chopping vegetables and fruit and using my hands to absorb the prana (life-force energy) of the raw foods.

When I feel busy, I remind myself there's enough time for everything that's important, and what could be more important than nourishing my body?

Eating healthy food is one of those things that gives time because fully nourished, we're better able to navigate the day feeling peaceful, energized and empowered. This is one of the most powerful acts of self-care we can engage in.

Try it! Fill up on love.

Today, your assignment is to cook and eat a meal with love. Give thanks for the raw ingredients, lovingly connect to the foods as you're combining them to make a meal, and give thanks before you eat.

You might offer a blessing such as, "May this food heal me from the inside out."

Eat slowly, mindfully, taking the time to really chew every bite and notice all the flavors mix in your mouth.

Take a minute after you eat and visualize all the vitamins and nutrients filtering through your body. Give thanks for the cycle of life, the Earth that gave you this food and even maybe everyone involved in the food chain, from the farmers who grew the food to the field hands who picked it to the truckers who transport it to the supermarket workers who unload, organize and check you out at the register.

Savor not only the food, but the time spent nourishing your body, your soul and your Earthly self.

If you're not sure where to find a recipe, Pinterest is a good place.

Another practice that's improved my relationship with food is to go recipe-less. I sort through my kitchen cabinets, and using my intuition, combine ingredients to create a meal unique to me.

This transforms the whole cooking experience into a time to connect to my higher self, be led by her, and then ingest the result in a beautiful, complete circle of life and love. Maybe it sounds a little woo woo, but give it a try! You'll feel the magic.

Journal prompts:

Today is an open invitation to examine your relationship with food and ask yourself — what does this relationship say about how worthy you feel of receiving nourishment, of taking the time to fuel up with healthy food? Where do any issues come from?

What message do any problems have for you, when viewed symbolically? What new story would you like to write?

If you tend to eat too much food, or crave specific foods, what are you really hungry for? For instance, craving sweets can sometimes indicate a desire for more sweetness in life. Carbs can indicate a desire for comfort.

How can you create more space to lovingly nurture yourself through food? What are you ready to heal in this area?

_____

_____

_____

_____

_____

_____

_____

_____

_____

_____

_____

_____

_____

_____

_____

_____

_____

_____

_____

_____

_____

_____

_____

_____

_____

_____

_____

_____

_____

_____

_____

_____

_____

_____

_____

_____

_____

_____

_____

_____

_____

_____

_____

_____

_____
_____
_____
_____
_____
_____
_____
_____
_____
_____
_____
_____
_____
_____
_____
_____
_____
_____
_____
_____
_____
_____
_____
_____
_____
_____
_____
_____
_____
_____

Integration

You made it! Congratulations on all the work you've done over the past four weeks.

It's time to integrate the undercurrents in the course to learn the truth of unconditional self-love.

You'll also explore what it means to create loving relationships that create space for your authentic self to thrive.

Day 29: Creating loving relationships.

This journey has been about loving yourself as you are so you can love others as they are. This was a self-love program, but obviously when we shift our insides, the outsides change, and this naturally affects relationships with those around us.

The more you love yourself and trust at the soul that you'll never abandon yourself, the less you'll feel the need to please others at your expense.

These changes can feel disorienting. Your first tentative steps may bring up fear or excitement, but for long-term evolution, it's important to be able to ride the ups and downs.

You may have a breakthrough and feel exhilarated in the moment, but then wonder if what you did was okay after the adrenaline rush ends. It's really important to hold strong and not backpedal.

Sit with the discomfort. Investigate it if you feel called using the tools you've learned in this journal such as working with past memories or simply asking yourself why you feel what you feel.

Let the pain or fear move through you until you return to peace and the truth of who you are, what you want, what you expect, and what you deserve.

Continue using the tools you've learned in this journal to heal in new and deeper ways. You have everything you need within you to heal and create new patterns. Affirm your right to assert yourself in the world. Over time it gets easier.

That said, today I want to give you a few additional tools to navigate relationships, along with the faith that your true blue ones will evolve with you, even if the other person isn't committed to personal growth. That's part of the magic here, that you can create better relationships just by changing your relationship with self.

Here are a few things to keep in mind:

1. We are all mirrors.

When someone makes you mad or triggers you, this only highlights unhealed parts of you.

Nothing can make you mad or sad or crazy unless the interaction highlighted an unhealed unaccepted, unintegrated part of you. (This does not include instances of abuse, of course.)

So when problems come up, the first step — even though it may seem counterintuitive — is to tune within.

Ask yourself questions like:

- Why is this bothering me so much?
- What other situations does this remind me of? Is there a pattern I need to address?
- What is my relationship with the emotion that's coming up? What message does this feeling have for me?
- What is coming up for healing or awareness?

2. Own your part in the conflict.

Conflicts take two. I know that can be hard to accept, but if you have an ongoing issue with someone, ask yourself where you're contributing to the problem.

Is there something you need to accept? Is there a boundary you need to set? A firm conversation? Where you are holding on to something that's not yours to hold on to?

An example from my life: I love things super organized. Mess drives me crazy. My husband, bless his heart, leaves piles of stuff everywhere. I feel like I'm constantly cleaning up after him.

This used to really bother me. Until I realized that I was being called to unconditionally accept him, just as he unconditionally accepted me.

I realized that this was a funny quirk of his, something that I would recall with laughter if God forbid something happened to him. So I decided to laugh about it now.

BUT I also decided that I had needs too — to have a clean house. So overtime we created designated sloppy areas. And I have just accepted that I clean more. Because I'm the one who cares about it — not him. I can't make him care about something he doesn't care about.

I'm not sure this was the perfect thing to do, but it worked for me. Yes, I still get frustrated, but I share this example, because I feel like with relationships, we tend to ask, should I accept this OR ask the other person to change, and I think the true answer is both.

I think every situation has enough variables to find a solution for the highest good. This is my truth. Find what feels good to you.

3. When you speak, share how you feel.

It's tempting to say things like, "you made me feel like this," but that closes down the conversation. It feels blame-y, gives your power away, and doesn't create space for authentic conversation.

Focus on I statements. "I feel like this when that happens." This is more vulnerable and requires you to tap into how you're truly feeling, which can be scary. But it's powerful and worth it.

You can also ask the other person, "How does that make you feel?" A lot of men aren't in tune with their feelings, but it never hurts to ask.

If the other person truly cares about you, they'll care about your feelings. Then the two of you can figure out a creative solution of the highest good, together.

In relationships, I've found it's a constant balance between letting go and standing firm.

Maintaining a constant inner awareness, asking yourself questions like:

- Where am I holding on too tightly?
- How can I let go?
- What is the solution of the highest good?
- How is this a relationship a mirror for things within me that I need to heal?
- How is and isn't this relationship serving me?

I've referenced my poor husband most of this time, but the same could also hold true for friendships, mothers, fathers and sisters, co-workers or anyone.

Relationships are our greatest teachers.

It's easy to turn away from difficulty, sweeping things under the rug. But the more we can sit with our own inner turmoil and understand why we are the way we are, the greater ability we'll have in navigating relationships with authenticity, personal power, and kindness.

I spent so many years of my life trying to make people care who didn't, and it was only because I didn't care about myself. I spent a lot of years overly flexible and lost myself in the process.

Speaking up for yourself can feel scary, but you can do it without the armor of using emotion as a manipulation tactic. Because sometimes we get upset in order to get what we want rather than simply asking from a place of power and confident expectation that our needs get to be met. Own your emotions, understand your emotions, and then ask for what you need powerfully, while still considering how it impacts the other person.

If at any point, you feel scared losing another person's love, tune into your heart, your body, and affirm your commitment to yourself. You have your own back. Remember that every ounce of pain is a call for love. Every challenging situation is an opportunity to heal more deeply, love more fearlessly and above all, live in a way that's unapologetically, fiercely you.

Journal prompts:

Take a moment to consider any relationship conflicts. If all relationships are a mirror, what unhealed parts of you do you think the relationships are reflecting?

Consider the areas where you feel like your needs are unmet in relationships. What does the balance of accepting others and standing up for your needs look like? In what ways are you afraid to speak up?

Looking at any conflicts from an elevated, 30,000-foot view. What can you see differently?

What do you need from your various relationships? How can you better support and show up for those you love? What other shifts do you feel called to make?

_____

_____

_____

_____

_____

_____

_____

_____

_____

_____

_____

_____

_____

_____

_____

_____

_____

_____

_____
_____
_____
_____
_____
_____
_____
_____
_____
_____
_____
_____
_____
_____
_____
_____
_____
_____
_____
_____
_____
_____
_____
_____
_____
_____
_____
_____
_____

_____

_____

_____

_____

_____

_____

_____

_____

_____

_____

_____

_____

_____

_____

_____

_____

_____

_____

_____

_____

_____

_____

_____

_____

_____

Day 30: Accessing the truth of unconditional love.

You did it! You devoted 30 days to exploring the highest potential of you. I'm so beyond proud of the work you've done. Today is all about honoring the truth of unconditional love.

All throughout this journal, you've been working to unwind limiting ideas of self, figure out which beliefs are yours and which you took on, where you've dimmed your light, and where you've sold yourself short by apologizing for who you are, not setting boundaries or speaking your truth.

You may have experienced breakthroughs and expanded in new ways, and that's awesome! That's what this is all about.

But unconditional self-love is also very much about honoring the struggle.

I'm all about letting it be easy, finding the path of least resistance, and letting go of everything that no longer serves you, but sometimes with growth, there comes an internal struggle. And that's okay.

It's selling yourself short to cling to suffering, but it's also selling yourself short to tell yourself not to struggle or to forcibly quiet internal turmoil, emotions or frustration to feel peaceful when you don't.

Frustration has immense gifts. It signals a breakthrough is right around the corner.

So I hope that with the tools you've learned in this program, from feeling your feelings to shadow work exercises to unwinding limiting beliefs and more, you lean into and work with your frustration. But I also hope that you give yourself the space to simply feel it.

Sometimes the subconscious has important messages for you, and it's important to create stillness, retreat into nature, spend time alone or in meditation, even for five minutes, to allow those messages to bubble up into your consciousness.

Resisting frustration or the struggle actually causes more of it. Ironically, the temptation is to resist struggle to feel peace, but this only causes more struggle.

Sometimes the purest pathway to peace is to embrace the frustration and the struggle. Open up to it and see what messages it contains for you.

Have faith in your own process and that your whole journey is a natural evolution toward greater love and connection.

Honor your cycles.

During the journal, we've talked about alignment and flow, and I briefly mentioned tuning into the energy of your life to see what's called for, but I'd like to take a little more time and address this today because it's really important.

Always tune in and feel your energy. Is it time for you to plant seeds? Sometimes when you're feeling frustrated looking for a result, it's a sign for you to plant more seeds, meaning take more small actions so you can taste the fruit of your desire.

Is it time for you to rest? Time to work hard? Time to float and not think about evolving or self-development? Or maybe it's a season of digging deep into internal inquiry and dissolving internal limitations holding you back.

The first year in my business, I got really burned out because I created non-stop, and instead of taking breaks when I was tired, I simply dug in and kept going.

I have so many ideas that it's hard to take a break, but I've come to realize that even if my mind doesn't fully shut off, it's still important to put the computer away and rest after taking intense action.

When I write in a very focused way, I feel tired afterward. It makes sense now — of course after putting intense energy into something I feel depleted afterward.

(Although some people talk about soul work energizing them, so maybe I judged myself for not feeling energized and tried to force myself into a feeling that wasn't mine.)

Now I consciously notice this and take breaks. Or if I find myself procrastinating, with little energy to complete important projects, I've come to realize that I'm not lazy. It's just that I'm not a robot and need time to recharge.

Nothing in nature blooms all year round.

It's easy to force ourselves, but it's very important to tune into our rhythms and honor them.

At the same time, if you find yourself consistently off or angry or tired, it could be a sign that you're not living in alignment or submerging a soul message or project that's trying to come through.

Then it's a call to rise up, tune in and take strong action to shift your life. Fatigue can indicate you're not living in alignment, that your body is working hard energetically as your consciousness represses a part of your true self. Sadness, anger — sometimes these emotions result from our responses to external circumstance, but they can also reflect how we're mistreating ourselves.

There's no step-by-step formula I can give you or concrete way to tell the difference. You are your own greatest intelligence. This is just a kind reminder to tune in, maybe in your journal or meditation, and ask questions like:

- How can I show up for myself in a better way?
- What do I need right now?
- If I was living in full alignment, what would that look like?

During these times of misalignment, it may be because you've shifted.

We're always evolving and need to shift our lives and habits, how we show up and express ourselves, maybe change our clothes or environment, decluttering or redecorating, to honor the new versions of ourselves that are emerging into the world.

We never fully arrive. A life lived on purpose, in dedication to your highest self, is one that honors your constant destruction and rebirth, struggle and ease, breakdown and breakthrough.

To treat yourself with love is to tune in to understand your processes and honor each as it's happening, never doubting your innate worthiness. Trust that if you follow the flow, everything will work out as it should.

Your entire purpose is to follow the flow. Honor your unfolding. It's not always easy, but what's actually hard and painful is living a life that's not yours, a life designed to please others all while killing your soul.

Love yourself enough to live *your* unique life. Your destiny. Your purpose. Your passion. Yes you'll have to learn lessons and heal and discard beliefs standing in the way, but that's what life is. A journey of transforming pain into passion and purpose.

Feel free to ask the universe for guidance. *Please show me a sign. What is my next step?*

You might find a book or a movie or a course or a teacher, even a conversation that gives you the insight you need to continue your journey. You might feel called to journal about your desires, or on the contrary, journal about where you're resisting and how you can let go. Maybe you'd love another Soul Scroll Journal!

Always take the next step no matter how small. Always believe in yourself no matter how hard it seems.

Always remember. You are a boundless sea of infinite light and love. This ocean of love doesn't exclude your darkness, your weaknesses and so-called flaws, but includes every part of you because every part of you is god(ess)-like and every part of you is worthy of love. Every part of you is love. And so it is.

Journal prompts:

What have been your biggest shifts / realizations throughout this program? What has been the biggest healing for you?

What new ideas have you picked up that you'd like to carry with you? What changes do you feel called to focus on going forward?

Finally, write yourself a thank you letter for your efforts over the past month. You've done a really amazing thing. Own it!

Alternatively, you could write a letter from the future you to the you now, sharing all the awesomeness that's in store if you keep fearlessly following your own path. Choose your adventure!

Feel free to take some time and read through your journal and honor the journey you just took.

_____
_____
_____
_____
_____
_____
_____
_____
_____
_____
_____
_____
_____
_____
_____
_____
_____
_____
_____
_____
_____
_____
_____
_____
_____
_____
_____
_____

_____
_____
_____
_____
_____
_____
_____
_____
_____
_____
_____
_____
_____
_____
_____
_____
_____
_____
_____
_____
_____
_____
_____
_____
_____
_____

The end!

Thank you so much for choosing Soul Scroll Journals as a guide through the galaxy of your inner world!

Our mission is to help you understand yourself so you can create a life as unique as you are.

We hope that you now feel more empowered to create a beautiful life of your choosing rather than the one you're programmed for or expected to live.

Please let us know how your experience was!

What's next:

1. Leave a review.
Did you love this journal? Share your thoughts on Amazon and let others know about your experience so their lives can also be transformed. This is how we change the world!

2. Download your bonus gifts at SoulScrollJournals.com/bonuses.
If you haven't already downloaded the Feeling Awareness meditation to help you connect to your heart and release painful emotions, go do that now!

3. Join the Soul Scroll Journal Family Facebook group!
Head to www.facebook.com/groups/soulscrolljournals to connect with others also on the path of creating an extraordinary life.

About Soul Scroll Journals

Everyone has a dream inside of them they're meant to live. Yet not everyone trusts themselves enough to create this dream and realize their destiny.

This is no small thing. The unique essence of you was created for a reason, and it will never exist again.

Too many people are held back because they don't know how to release past pain, find the answers within, and trust themselves to create the extraordinary life they're meant to live.

Too many people are so full of external information and well-meaning but ultimately noisy advice that they've lost connection to their own hearts.

We wanted to inspire dreamers to put down their phones and scroll their souls.

To find the vision within and connect to the heartfelt guidance to create it, one day at a time.

That's why Soul Scroll Journals were born. The journals are your friend and unbiased guide to help you connect to your heart, clarify your dreams and desires, and teach you how to use your intuition to create it.

They'll help you become the person you were always meant to be — right now.

Download a free, powerful meditation to release past pain and connect to your heart at SoulScrollJournals.com/bonuses.

Other Soul Scroll Journals

Play with the Day yearly goal journal

Cast a vision. Set monthly intentions. Live with soul.

Play with the Day is a soulful goal journal and habit tracker that will hep you live better — not just get more done.

With it, you'll weave beautiful rituals and habits into your life along with a few focused to-do's, leaving plenty of room for play.

You'll live more soulfully while tapping into the universe's magic to help you become who you most want to be.

Because life isn't about checking things off a list — it's about living!

Listen to Your Heart guided journal

Your heart is always guiding you to a life you love. This journal will help you hear these important messages.

Listen to Your Heart guided journal will support you through short daily readings and thought-provoking journal prompts to get crystal clear on what you want while releasing everything holding you back from creating it.

The good news is that feeling stuck is actually a powerful threshold inviting you to create a whole new vision for your life.

Listen to Your Heart will help you get clear on exactly who you are and what you want.

Find these journals and more at SoulScrollJournals.com.